TOWARD
ACCOUNTABLE
TEACHERS

TOWARD ACCOUNTABLE TEACHERS

Their Appraisal and Improvement

John D. McNeil
University of California, Los Angeles

HOLT, RINEHART AND WINSTON, INC.
New York   Chicago   San Francisco   Atlanta
Dallas   Montreal   Toronto   London   Sydney

Preface

This book is written for teachers—both novice and experienced—who want to study their teaching so they need not be ashamed and for those supervisors in colleges and in school systems who have responsibility for helping teachers become more effective with pupils and who want to be fair in their assessment of teachers. School board members and administrators should regard the ideas presented as timely responses to the concern that unfit teachers are depriving pupils of their right to educational progress.

A central aim in *Toward Accountable Teachers* is to remedy an imbalance: to allow the criterion of pupil progress, rather than the subjective factors which now operate in the evaluation of teachers, to become part of the basis upon which teachers are judged. Recent knowledge of pedagogy (curriculum and instruction) has been cast into a self-corrective system for assessing and improving the teacher's classroom behavior, and new intellectual tools—such as "criterion-referenced tests," "learning for mastery," "performance or behavioral objectives," and "contract decision making"—are explained and related to a tested model for the supervising of teachers. The reader will find in the text practical procedures for identifying strengths and weaknesses of teachers and will learn about specific courses of action for overcoming the teacher's instructional deficiencies.

December 1970   **John D. McNeil**

Contents

Chapter   3
Supervision by Objectives   33

Chapter   4
Four Phases in the Improvement of Instruction   49

Chapter   5

Technical Qualifications for Those Participating in the Improvement of Instruction   79

Chapter   6

Applying Supervision by Objectives in Student Teaching   103

TOWARD ACCOUNTABLE TEACHERS

chapter 1

WANTED: A NEW APPROACH
TO THE ASSESSMENT
OF TEACHERS
AND THE IMPROVEMENT
OF INSTRUCTION

Sometimes a tool is invented and one has to search for its applications: the small boy who finds his first hammer loses no time in finding things that need hammering. Other times there are serious problems for which we must seek adequate answers, as in the matter of evaluating teachers. Teacher evaluation is troublesome, but fortunately there is a workable solution, and it is clear that society in general and professional educators in particular are ready for a practical response to the problems of how to appraise one's ability to teach and how best to help a teacher improve his instruction.

LOSS OF CONFIDENCE IN SCHOOL PROGRAMS OF EVALUATION

Current practices in evaluating teachers are shocking. National surveys (NEA, 1964, 1969) have revealed that only about half the school systems in the United States follow any formal procedures in evaluating their teachers, and the procedures used are most inadequate. Written ratings are typically required for probationary teachers, less frequently for teachers with continuous contracts, and the principal is nearly always responsible for these evaluations. Indirect methods used in collecting data about a teacher's effectiveness include: gathering impressions of him outside the classroom; noting his professional activities; gathering impressions of him from pupils and from the appearance of the classroom; studying pupil achievement records; and listening to what parents and other teachers say about him. Although three out of four superintendents and principals express confidence in their program of evaluation, *one half* of their teachers do not. The procedures used as a basis for evaluation are considered unfair—pupil achievement records don't always take into account the fact that a teacher has had a particularly unruly class; reports from parents are too subjective; and the teacher's professional activity may be unrelated to his work with pupils. The direct method of observing teaching in the classroom is infrequently used and is seldom conducted on a regular schedule. Teachers in secondary schools receive fewer observations than those in elementary schools. Only about 34 percent of secondary school teachers are observed while teaching even once for a period of five minutes or longer during the year. The median number of observations received by those in elementary schools is two; in secondary schools, one. Only half of these observations are followed by a conference with the observer.

Representatives of teacher organizations are concerned about the present system of evaluation, making such statements as, "Principals with large numbers of teachers to be rated drop into a teacher's room for a ten-minute visit and subsequently fill out forms which state in detail not only their estimate of the teacher's competence but also his personal qualifications" (Segure, 1966). Leaders of organized teachers are calling for arrangements by which teachers themselves can participate in upholding standards of teaching among their peers. Some are now advocating more self-evaluation, whereby the individual teacher analyses his own performance and selects aspects of his behavior for improvement. However, since it has not been shown how experienced teachers will overcome the weaknesses now present in the conduct of observations by principals, department chairmen, and supervisors, there is no assurance that teachers will be more likely to make warranted judgments than have supervisors. And it has not been demonstrated that self-evaluation leads to the identification and removal of the most crucial deficiencies in one's teaching.

Members of boards of education and teacher organizations recognize that a major problem of the school system is how to weed out the unfit teacher. Rather than attempt to prove at a hearing that a teacher is unsatisfactory—and risk that his judgment will be questioned by his superiors—a principal will often give that teacher a satisfactory rating and then encourage him to transfer to another school. The transfer is rationalized on the grounds that a teacher who does not work out in one school may do better in another where the conditions are different, but too often this tactic merely shifts the problem without resolving it.

Two duties are commonly assigned to the principal by the school superintendent: (1) to assess teachers, indicating in the case of those in probationary status whether or not the district should retain them and (2) to help teachers improve instructionally. Principals believe they can do the first and, as we have seen, do so by reflecting upon personality and inferences collected from many sources. These inferences are drawn more from the teacher's participation in staff affairs, activity in school organizations, and public relations than from observations related to valid judgment about instructional effectiveness in the classroom.

Most principals do not give much time to the second task, instructional improvement of the teacher in the classroom. The school principal with a large staff will say there are not enough hours in the day to allow him to spend time with each teacher individually, analyzing instruction and devising new instructional strategies. Further, he has other essential tasks, for instance, the duty of building teacher morale, which often calls for individual conferences that are tangential to the teacher's work with pupils. As a school and community leader the principal must contribute time and energy to parents and other community persons, and as a manager of a large enterprise he has responsibility for written communications, keeping of accounts, scheduling of activities, and the supervision of nonteaching personnel. Also, the principal wants to maintain a personal contact with as many of the students in the school as possible, showing his interest in them and guiding their activities in a direction consistent with school policy. Consequently, responsibility for close supervision of the teacher in the classroom is often given to a department chairman, to a central office supervisor representing a subject-matter field, or to an assistant principal—a person who faces many of the same conflicting demands for time that the principal experiences.

Most principals, even those in elementary schools, will admit that curricular changes in the fields of mathematics, science, language arts, reading, and social studies have been so fundamental and rapid that the principal no longer presumes to have sufficient knowledge of content and method to qualify as a teaching specialist in these fields. Without expertise in a particular subject, a principal is reluctant to work with the teacher in improving the teaching of that subject matter.

The principal's role in instructional improvement needs redefining, and he is entitled to learn new skills with which to carry out his role. He *can* be effective in improving the instruction of his teachers but not by continuing to act as most principals have been accustomed to acting. Fortunately, a new role has been defined and made operational—principals who fulfill it find that they can in fact be instructional leaders in their schools and that this responsibility is compatible with other duties. In later chapters, this new role, as it applies to principals and others, will be described.

DISCONTENT ON THE PART OF BOARD MEMBERS

There is a variety of explanations for the actions of school board members with respect to teacher assessment. The school board member wants to be assured that the superintendent is differentiating among teachers in order that the district will select and retain those who can best help pupils attain the expectations of the community. Practically, he wants administrators to identify differences among teachers so that monies for salaries (which amount to about 80 percent of a school system's budget) can be spent wisely. Board members believe that it is grossly inefficient to reward all teachers equally when their productivity is not equal, and they know that longevity of service is no indicator of instructional productivity. The school board member is unwilling to accept the assumption that all teachers are equally competent to teach just because they have a license or a credential and is frustrated when the superintendent or principal makes the opposite assumption, that all licensed teachers are competent and, therefore, the best way to improve instruction is to give more money (or released time, smaller classes, or other fringe benefits) to teachers so they can perform more consistently with their potential. The board member would like to give more money to those who contribute more and to reward those teachers who have made a practical difference in the lives of pupils.

UNFAIR EVALUATION OF THOSE PREPARING TO TEACH

Charges against college supervisors of student teachers and interns are similar to those leveled at supervisors in school systems. The college supervisor seldom has a pre-observational conference with these novice teachers before a lesson is presented, and there is often a conflict between the expectations of the college supervisor and the master teacher in the classroom where the student teacher is doing his teaching. The training teacher or master teacher is not explicit in defining the competencies which the student teacher must acquire from his training: performance objectives which define these competencies have rarely been prepared; there is no sequencing of the order in which these competencies are to be won; and there seldom is a systematic ordering of experiences necessary for achieving desired changes in the student teacher. A second assignment for a student teacher may be little more than a reiteration of what has already been learned in the first assignment rather than part of a planned program by which teaching skills are expanded. A frequent result is that the novice teacher does not improve from one assignment to another.

Since rating scales used to assess student teachers lack objectivity, the use of the scales often reveals the characteristics and prejudices of the rater—the master teacher or college supervisor—rather than giving an accurate description of the student teacher's work with pupils.

Sorenson's (1967) study of practice teaching provides evidence of subjective evaluations. Sorenson asked 163 student teachers to "list the things you would tell your best friend to do in order to get a grade of 'A' from your present training teacher." The responses indicated that a high rating was perceived as *more* dependent upon (1) doing as one was told; (2) fawning or cultivating the supervisor (having coffee with her and saying things like, "I think that was a very good idea, Mrs. _____") ; (3) preparing lesson plans in advance; (4) keeping absolute control of the class at all times; (5) using an inductive approach in teaching; (6) giving extremely explicit directions; and (7) being original. Sorenson's data seem to support the following generalization: sources most likely to yield information about the ultimate measure of the teacher's effectiveness—impact upon the student—are least likely to be used.

chapter **2**

THE GREAT CHANGE IN THE CONCEPT OF TEACHING

Appraisal and improvement of teaching require a definition of good teaching, because priorities among criteria are changing. Achievement of pupils in desired and desirable ways is a much more valuable indicator that good teaching has taken place than the actions of teachers independent of consequences on learners. Methods of teaching are not to be prized but appraised.

CHANGE FROM ASCRIPTION TO RESULTS

Sociologists speak of certain occupations as having ascriptive positions, meaning by this that the holder of the position attained and maintains his job on categorical grounds rather than on the basis of achievement. Devoting many class hours to preparation or displaying great effort in a task would be examples of categorical grounds. However just because one has participated in course work or worked hard does not mean that he has achieved. Most occupations do have their ascriptive features. The minister, for instance, has been expected categorically to perform the sacraments in a given manner, and not to do so would bring a negative evaluation. On the other hand, salesmen are primarily expected to achieve. Categorical efforts are not enough: salesmen must sell, not merely carry out recommended procedures for selling. Many professions are moving from an emphasis upon ascription to an emphasis upon results—there is less concern about *how* someone goes about his work but much more interest in *what* follows from this activity. For example, the minister is now not only judged by the way he delivers his sermon but by whether or not he has made a noticeable difference in the conduct of life around him. Recently a campus minister was criticized by students, because there was little evidence that his parishioners were changing their behavior as a result of his sermons. Reflecting the older notion of ascription, this minister replied, "Look, my job is not to shape behavior but to share the 'good news.' " Similarly, teaching has been an ascribed profession. Teachers were valued for displaying certain qualities, ranging from kinds of language to specifications of handwriting, tone of voice, and manner of dress, whether or not they achieved results. The failure to educate all students and the massive academic retardation which exists, especially among minority-group students, has brought home the fact that one cannot judge a teacher as good solely because he is following recommended procedures or meets categorical expectations. It is becoming essential to note the consequences of procedures and personal qualities upon learners: if the learners are not progressing as desired, the teacher has not been successful even if he meets ascribed requirements.

CHANGE FROM VALUING METHODS
TO NOTING EFFECTS OF METHODS

The most serious criticism of prevailing practice in teacher evaluation has arisen out of opposition to experiments on humans. Teachers have been accused of being unwilling to test the efficacy of their instruction and have, therefore, violated the ethics required of those who have been given responsibility for others, be they patients or learners. It is not always recognized that every lesson is an experiment on learners. As phrased by Bixler, "The ethical question before us today is: 'What responsibilities do we have to the human beings with whom we experiment? What responsibilities do we have to mankind to carry out studies of the effectiveness of our favorite, but largely untested methods of teaching?' " (Bixler, 1966).

A large school system had for years rated certain of its teachers as outstanding teachers of reading. When, for a number of reasons, the school district was forced to examine the progress of pupils in their ability to read, it was discovered that the majority of pupils under the direction of highly rated teachers had not learned to read. How could a teacher be judged outstanding when pupils were not achieving? The answer was simple. The teacher was being judged by the extent to which an ascribed role—in this case a method for teaching reading—was being followed. Did the teacher have three reading groups? Were the wall charts at the right height? Were the children using *On Cherry Street* at the right time of year? Affirmative answers to questions of teaching procedure constituted successful teaching more than pupil attainment of specified competence in reading. Only now, in a climate of assessment, is the school district beginning to move from valuing of a particular *method* for teaching to attending to the results of that method and other methods which are being introduced. The superintendent now says to the teacher, "You are not required to follow a set of lock-stepped procedures. You are free to design instructional strategies, to use a variety of materials and approaches— but you are expected to get results."

SLOW PROGRESS TOWARD MEASUREMENT OF INSTRUCTION THROUGH RESULTS

As early as 1897, Joseph Mayer Rice, a pioneer among students of education, reported to the school superintendents of America his investigation of spelling in the school systems of several cities, showing that children who had spent 40 minutes a day in studying spelling did not spell any better than children in the schools of other cities where they devoted only 10 minutes a day to that study. His presentation threw the assemblage into dismay and indignant protest. The opposition was not directed against the method and findings of the investigator, but against the investigator, who had pretended to measure the results of teaching spelling by testing the ability of the children to spell.

Fifteen years later, Ayers cited the above incident as a benchmark of change, stating that the same association of school superintendents had now agreed to the basic proposition that the effectiveness of the school, the methods, and the teachers must be measured by the results secured (Ayers, 1912). Ayers was premature in his conclusion that "How much?," "How many?," and "With what result?" were going to replace guesswork, imagination, and oratory as criteria for shaping educational policy. School practice did not follow what he saw as the signs of more efficient education—efforts to specify what the product is, to define standards, to see that teachers produce what they say they are, and to determine the ratio of product and time. Instead of being judged with knowledge, methods of instruction continued to be valued on the basis of speculation, tradition, opinion, and theory.

A study by Arthur Boyce of methods for measuring teachers' efficiency was published in the 1915 *NSSE Yearbook* (Boyce, 1915). Boyce revealed that two classes of methods for rating teachers were in use. One was the *general impression method* which was not really a method but a variety of approaches whereby judgments were not controlled by an outline of factors, a definition, or rules of any kind. Teachers were "rated" as good, bad, or indifferent, as worthy or unworthy of retention and promotion, according to the opinion of the one who judged them, but there was nothing to tell what the judgment really meant, because no evidence was presented to support the final rating. A second approach was the *analytical method*, a rating scheme which attempted to analyze the particulars in which teachers were superior or inferior. Among the most popular qualities considered were discipline, instructional skill, scholarship, cooperation and loyalty, plan and method, personality, professional interest, manner, voice, daily preparation, accuracy and promptness, professional training and preparation, attitude toward children, appearance and health, routine. Few of the schemes defined the terms used in analyzing the teachers, and the schemes did not eliminate *mere* personal opinion. Boyce proposed an improved method for guiding the rating of teachers, a plan that avoided vague and all-inclusive terms, such as "personality" and "scholarship." He organized the qualities of teachers under the five headings: (1) "personal equipment," which included accuracy, tact, and physical, mental, and moral qualities; (2) "social equipment" which was meant to cover several qualities important to the children, the community, and the profession, for example, use of English; (3) "school management," which had to do with such routine factors as care of the room and handling of classes; (4) "techniques of teaching," including clearness of aim, skill in developing habit formation, skill in stimulating thought, skill in questioning, skill in teaching how to study, and so on; and (5) results as shown by response of the class, pupil progress in the subject matter and in general development, and moral influence. Examination of rating scales in use today (see Figure 1) shows that there has been little change from that proposed in 1915 by Boyce and perhaps even a decrease in emphasis on results.

THE ORGANIZED PROFESSION AND THE RATING OF TEACHERS

The organized profession has generally opposed rating. The Association for Supervision and Curriculum Development (ASCD) in 1950 set forth an alternative to rating teachers, based on the opinions of members of ASCD, classroom teachers, and other professionals, which was described in the publication *Better Than Rating* (ASCD, 1950). Two chief arguments were advanced by the commission that developed this publication: (1) techniques of rating are detrimental to teachers—when being rated, the teacher is unhappy, insecure, uncertain, unwilling to attempt new things, and unable to accomplish the best results in work with children; and (2) administrative or supervisory rating of teachers is undemocratic. The commission preferred to emphasize the professional improvement of the teacher and gave slight attention to identifying those who should be guided out of the profession. The members admitted that, in rare instances, discharge might be warranted if the teacher was emotionally unstable, unable to work with others in group settings, expressed dissatisfaction, and would not develop into a creative and capable teacher. However, what would constitute evidence that negative judgments were warranted was not spelled out.

The ASCD document is important, because it reveals the underlying assumption of professional policy with respect to teacher assessment. In my opinion, the ideas expressed overemphasize the school system's responsibility for personal development and protection of the teacher and do not give enough consideration to the pupil's welfare. From reading the document, one can easily get the impression that the purpose of the school is to advance the well-being of teachers. Professional leaders seem to have assumed that learners will be better served if teachers become more self-directed, become more mature (because of improved status and security in group activities), and reach their own personal goals. In other words, teachers are pictured as asking for a "blank check"—anything that serves their interest is in the interest of pupils! Although members of the ASCD commission believed that steps necessary to the development of an appraisal plan could not be outlined in advance or in isolation from the local situation where the plan was to operate, they did offer such guidelines as:

1. The plan should be developed through the involvement of pupils, school personnel, and lay citizens.
2. Methods and procedures of appraisal should be evolved by the groups which use them.
3. Techniques should be developed for patterning evidence of individual growth and development.
4. The school community should provide its teachers with a variety of opportunities for professional growth, opportunities to work on problems which they feel to be important, to

attend conferences and national meetings, to visit other schools, and to have their tuition paid for professional courses.

TEACHER ORGANIZATIONS AND THEIR FAILURE TO WEED OUT THE UNFIT TEACHER

Will teacher organizations seek objective criteria for evaluating performance and weeding out the unfit teacher?

Figure 1 A TYPICAL PROBATIONARY TEACHER EVALUATION FORM

This form is composed of some selected general descriptions of activities which relate to district philosophy of what is a good teacher. It is to be used as a guide sheet to aid the evaluator in observing and evaluating teacher performance objectively and fairly. It is hoped that this instrument will contribute positively to programs of improvement of instruction and selection of competent staff.

Evaluator estimates and appraisals of instructor performance are indicated by the following symbols:

A—Interpret instructor performance as reflecting outstanding ability in this area (Satisfactory to District)

E—Interpret instructor performance as reflecting strength in this area (Satisfactory to District)

S—Interpret instructor performance as reflecting satisfactory progress in this area (Satisfactory to District)

N—Interpret instructor performance as reflecting a need for improvement in this area (Unsatisfactory to District)

Figure 1 (continued)

Left Blank—Had no opportunity to observe performance relating to this area

Where "N" ratings are given in this area, examples of
instructor behaviors relating with this area must be recorded. Behavior reflecting special strength in an area
may be recorded in some instances for the purpose of
instructor commendation. (Where examples are cited, be
descriptive and specific and indicate whether or not they
are typical of the instructor. Record exactly what happened in a situation, not merely your reaction to what
happened.)

A. Evaluation of the teaching-learning situation:

1. I observe techniques of *lesson presentation* which
    I think to be well executed, understanding that
    there are various acceptable methods, techniques
    and philosophies of sound education. (I note fac-
    tual or theoretical evidence that students learn
    from teacher's techniques: laboratory or shop
    demonstration and supervision methods, lectures,
    discussions, questioning, panels, committees, etc.)
    ⎯⎯⎯⎯

2. I evaluate teaching *planning and organization* of
    class activities as adequate. (I note evidence of
    teacher use of out-of-class time in preparation of
    courses of study, demonstration materials, labora-
    tory materials, lecture notes, syllabi to students,
    examinations, etc.)   ⎯⎯⎯⎯

3. I observe *student motivation and class control*
    techniques which I believe appropriate to the par-
    ticular learning situation, understanding that
    there are various acceptable methods and tech-
    niques, and differing levels of student maturity

Figure 1 (continued)

    (student participates in an active, positive and responsible way in learning situation). _____

4. I evaluate teacher direction of *lesson-connected out-of-class learning activities* as being adequate, understanding that there are various acceptable methods, techniques and philosophies of sound education (lesson assignments, papers, reports, field trips, projects, etc.). _____

5. I evaluate teacher's *learning-evaluation* techniques as being adequate, understanding that there are various acceptable methods, techniques, and philosophies of sound education (tests, grading practices, etc.). _____

6. I observe *personal characteristics* of this teacher which I believe will contribute to his success in the teaching-learning situation (voice, mannerisms, etc.). _____

7. I evaluate the use of *teaching aids* as being appropriate to the lesson and to the nature of the class (audiovisual aids, blackboard diagrams, community resources, etc.). _____

8. I evaluate teacher concern for *physical conditions* of the teaching situation as adequate. _____

B. Evaluation of professional preparation of teacher:

1. I evaluate this teacher as having adequate depth and breadth of *subject matter preparation* (knowledge of fact, detail and relationship concepts in fields, craftsmanship, etc.). _____

2. I evaluate this teacher's knowledge of *related subject matter* areas to be adequate to enable him to make the subject matter meaningful to students (use of examples, parallels, etc.). _____

3. I evaluate that this teacher's knowledge is re-

Figure 1 (continued)

flected well in the *course content and organization* (gives more than a repeat of text materials, etc.). _____

C. Evaluation of teacher's cooperation with administrative policies, directives and clerical requirements:

1 I believe this teacher has adequately met *administrative clerical needs* (attendance and grade records filled out properly and turned in on time, text and library book requests completed, etc.). _____
2. I believe this teacher has carried out satisfactorily *special assignments and departmental duties.* _____

3. I believe this teacher has satisfactory concern for the care of *school property.* _____

D. Evaluation of teacher's professional development:

1. I interpret teacher activity as representing continuing effort toward *professional improvement* (additional course work, attendance at workshops and conferences, independent research or study, personal library, articles or papers in field published or presented, etc.). _____
2. I interpret teacher activity as representing a contribution to the *further improvement of teaching as a profession* (membership and activity in professional organizations, participation in committees of local professional organizations, papers and reports in field published, etc.). _____

E. Other comments:

(Any general comments concerning the teacher, the teaching situation, or other)

The full settlement of the 1969 New York City teachers' contract with the Board of Education contains a provision, titled "accountability," treating teacher competencies. Both the Board and the union agreed to join in an effort in cooperation with universities, community school boards, and parent organizations to develop objective criteria of professional accountability. The union seemed to recognize the need to do something about those teachers in the system whose performance is wanting. Albert Shanker, the president of the United Federation of Teachers, admitted that there are within a system the size of New York some teachers who obviously shouldn't be there. The fact is that, in this New York system of between 30,000 and 40,000 regular teachers, only about a dozen are let go each year because of incompetence, and in this respect New York is not much different from Chicago, Los Angeles, and other large cities. A major reason for the failure in the past to act against incompetents is as the new contract provision implies, the lack of objective criteria for evaluating performance.

There are now more public statements being made to the effect that as teacher salaries increase their productivity and efficiency should increase too. Increasingly, one hears that the question of teacher productivity must be faced, that teacher organizations should mount a major program of self-examination, and that with every demand for better salaries, teachers should submit a corresponding design for increased teacher efficiency. For instance, in a new study entitled *Teachers for the Real World*, one reads, "Much is written about the self-esteem and commitment of teachers, but until the teaching profession establishes its own self-government and sets its own pattern of performance and evaluation there will be too little commitment" (Smith and others, 1969). Helen Bain, President of the National Education Association, has forthrightly identified an internal problem associated with the demand for teacher accountability, saying, "Teachers are reluctant to make peer judgments in the public interest. With self-governance, they will have to face up to this responsibility. It doesn't necessarily mean judging peers in one's own administrative jurisdiction. It does mean we develop a sophisticated understanding of competence, ethics, due process, and the public welfare" (Bain, 1970). And in the article, "A New Approach to Merit Rating of Teachers" (1968), Anthony reported that teaching experience in years is not related significantly either to pupil achievement or to classroom environment, suggesting that seniority as a criterion for reward be deemphasized.

CRITERIA FOR IDENTIFYING
THE EFFECTIVE INSTRUCTOR

A criterion is a standard for judging, and the criteria of teacher effectiveness should be derived from the goals of the educational system. Since in any system there are usually several goals, it is unlikely that there will be a single concrete and universal criterion for teacher ability. As Gage says, "The criterion of teacher effectiveness betokens a degree of generality that has seldom been found in any branch of the behavioral sciences" (Gage, 1968). It is even doubtful that there exists a single variable of instruction that applies to all of teaching for all pupils, in all subject matters and for all objectives. Joseph Morsh and Eleanor Wilder prepared one of the most comprehensive reviews of the literature concerning the problems associated with teacher effectiveness (Morsh and Wilder, 1953). Their examination and critical analysis of over 900 references showed the popularity and worth of certain criteria, for example:

1. *Administrative ratings.* Administrative over-all opinion constitutes the most widely used measure of instructional competence. For the most part, these ratings do not produce very high correlations with measures of student gain. Ratings made by the same person are apt to be contaminated by halo.

2. *Peer ratings.* Peer ratings have been little used. In using peer opinions, ranks will probably give better results than ratings. Halo influences peer ratings just as it does administrative ratings.

3. *Student ratings.* The use of student ratings appears to be growing. Such ratings tend to show fair consistency. Considerable halo effect is usually found when students rate their instructors on several traits. Results may indicate that if the instructor favors the brighter students he will be approved by them. If the teacher is for the weaker students, he will be disapproved of by the brighter students.

4. *Self-ratings.* There is some tendency for instructors to overrate themselves. Self-rating shows negligible relationships with administration ratings, student ratings, or measures of student gain.

5. *Systematic observation.* Most of the observations have been dependent upon the subjective judgment of the observer. No single, specific, observable teacher act has yet been found whose frequency is invariably significantly connected with student achievement.

6. *Student gains.* Of the several methods used to measure student change, residual student gain (the difference between actual gain and predicted gain) is becoming more widely used as a criterion of an instructor's effectiveness. It appears to offer one of the best criteria thus far used.

EVALUATION OF INSTRUCTION IN COLLEGES AND UNIVERSITIES

Colleges and universities frequently ask that promotion committees assess a candidate's teaching as well as his research and public service. In judging effectiveness, these faculty committees try to consider such points as the following: command of subject; ability to organize his material and to present it with logic and force; capacity to awaken in students an awareness of the relationship of his subject to other fields of knowledge; spirit and enthusiasm; ability to arouse curiosity in beginning students and to stimulate advanced students to creative work. The committees are supposed to indicate the source of evidence on which the appraisal has been based. Evidence may include the opinion of other members of the candidate's department, of students, and of graduates who have achieved notable professional success since leaving the institution and the development of new and effective techniques of instruction. However, there is dissatisfaction with the assessment procedures used in higher education. Increasingly, those in college are recognizing that good teaching is not a phenomenon, but a class of diverse phenomena, with various criteria and sometimes incompatible traits. In making awards for distinguished teaching, committees have come to appreciate the diversity of teaching types and approaches, the diversity of calibre and motivation of the students, and hence the nonequivalence of effort, of successful product, and of criteria for the several useful forms of teaching. Students are more active than before in conducting informal polls and ratings of professors and in collecting subjective comments on what they think are weaknesses and strengths of professors. The chancellor of the University of California at Riverside has publicly endorsed a new policy requiring student evaluation of professors before they can be promoted.

In their monograph "Measuring Faculty Performance" (1969), Arthur Cohen and Florence Brawer point out that most evaluation of faculty is based on personality and behavior, mistakenly equating both with teaching effectiveness. Measuring teacher behavior without measuring student learning will do little to improve instruction, and Cohen and Brawer propose using student gain as a measure of teacher effectiveness, adding that it is gain with respect for the objects of the course which should be measured.

THE BIG "T" AND THE LITTLE "t" IN TEACHING

It is clear that the ideal of great teaching is in the eye of the beholder. The diagram below shows examples of the kinds of qualities that have been sought, for example, personality variables such as intelligence and emotional stability; preparation—courses taken and grades; political factors—religion, race; and physical standards such as vision and freedom from contagious disease. Many of these qualities are valued by particular local communities; not all are universally sought. One school principal may want a teacher who will rock the boat, generating new approaches and challenging the status quo. Another will desire teachers who conform and maintain the established routine. "Big T" concepts of the good teachers exist and will continue to exist; as desired qualities, they vary from school to school. It is important, however, to notice that one competency in teaching is indispensable, necessary if not sufficient. This critical dimension of teaching is shown in Figure 2 as little "t." It refers to the teacher's ability to formulate instructional objectives (intents), and to design and execute instructional sequences which enable pupils to reach these objectives.

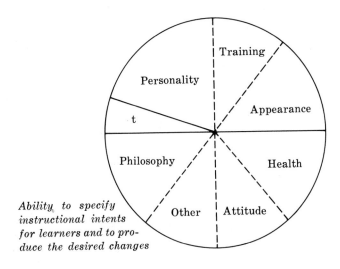

Figure 2

Wherever there is a teacher-learner relationship, the learner has the right to expect his teacher to bring about specific competencies in him, the learner.

The central importance of pedagogical ability—little "t"—must be given more attention in our assessment programs. It is true that the teacher has responsibilities in areas other than the classroom, obligations to: (a) the community—to work with parents and civic groups; (b) the school as an institution—to accept duties that enhance the operation of the school as a whole and to cooperate with fellow staff members; (c) his own personal life—to improve his mental and physical condition. It has been argued that the teacher's advancement in these areas, which are peripheral to the teaching act, may have much to do with success in his pedagogical role. We don't have to guess about this, however, if primary attention is given to the pedagogical effectiveness of the teacher. If a teacher at first cannot produce desired change or progress of learners and subsequent help is given to that teacher, the value of that help to performance in the classroom is demonstrated by whether or not the desired pupil progress follows.

PEDAGOGICAL EFFECTIVENESS: THE METHOD OF INFLUENCE AND A BEHAVIORAL MODEL OF TEACHING

Most of the teacher's actions within the classroom can be characterized as influence; that is, the teacher presents opportunities, activities, or learning experiences to the pupils without being able to state specifically how learners are to be changed as a result of these activities. The teacher may feel that the activities are valuable in themselves—that they are enjoyable, are part of our heritage, and will perhaps move the learner in desirable (but unspecified in advance) ways. In short, the method of influence is to select activities because of aesthetic quality, availability, tradition, or other factors and because the teacher "hopes" that something good will follow their use. The teacher who plays the "Nutcracker Suite" without being able to specify how the learners are to be different as a result of hearing the music is engaging in influence, not teaching.

In contrast, a behavioral or performance definition of teaching as pedagogy makes use of a means-ends distinction. The activity is not prized so much for its own sake (an end) but as a means to some specific end. According to the pedagogical or behavioral concept of teaching, the teacher gives more attention to defining what learners should be able to do *after* instruction, specifying in advance what responses the learners cannot now make but will be able to make in the presence of some situation or class of situations. This constitutes the instructional intent or end sought. Activities or sequences of instruction are then selected and ordered to produce this effect, and these are only judged as successful when the intended effect occurs in the learner. By this definition, teaching is the specification of desired changes in learners, the ordering of instructional events to produce the changes, and the actual attainment of the changed behavior by the learner. If the learning does not occur as intended, there has been no successful teaching.

Specifying the changes sought reduces much ambiguity and thus makes possible better planning and evaluation of instruction. A precise statement of outcomes gives clues to what kind of instructional sequence will be most effective, and with clear objectives the teacher is able to measure learner's attainment and make inferences about both the learner's performance and the instruction given.

Evidence continues to show that learning is more effective if the expected outcomes are clear to the learners (Dalis, 1968). There are also data indicating that teaching for specific learner gains produces greater achievement than the method of influence, which does not have predetermined results as the criterion of teaching effectiveness (Wittrock, 1962; Silberman, 1964; Smithman, 1970). In spite of its demonstrated advantages to the learner, the behavioral change concept of teaching does not constitute the prevalent manner in which classroom instruction is carried out; the method of influence—exposure to a variety of activities—still predominates.

Although teaching for results is increasing, it is unlikely that the method of influence will be completely eliminated, nor should it. The method of influence has the advantage of giving the teacher respite from the intellectual task of relating means and ends, and as consumations rather than instrumental acts, the activities can indeed be pleasurable to participants and may serve to reinforce prior learnings. Further, it is possible to present instructional activities without having objectives in advance and to observe what changes in pupils follow from these activities; such observation often brings needed objectives to the attention of the teacher. The point I would like to make is that, in addition to using the method of influence, teachers must teach for specific behavioral changes in learners and accept accountability for their teaching actions in terms of whether or not the desired changes occur. Those concerned with appraisal and improvement of teachers must give more weight to the pedagogical effectiveness of a teacher as demonstrated by progress shown by pupils. In making a decision regarding the retention of a teacher, more attention must be given to evidence of the teacher's ability to effect desirable changes in learners. To date this evidence has not been systematically gathered; hence less defensible criteria are used in making decisions regarding teacher retention.

Teachers can improve in their ability to produce learning in pupils if pupil progress becomes a matter of emphasis. Pupils are better served when we focus on teaching in relation to pupils rather than solely on the teacher, who after all is only an enabling mediator in the classroom: schools exist for pupils, not teachers. Parochial and extraneous criteria for judging teacher effectiveness will always be present, but should be balanced with evidence of effects upon learners. Parents, peers, and principal will respond to the everyday conduct of teachers which pleases or annoys them, and sometimes their emotional feelings will be communicated. It has been said that "the purpose of evaluation is to convey feeling," but there is a rational complement to this release of subjective feeling which is often devastating to the recipient. A rational approach makes greater use of factual data, employs more subtle forms of analysis, and justifies recommendations regarding instruction by demonstrating the effect of these recommended practices upon pupils, not relying on the personal authority of the supervisor.

chapter **3**

SUPERVISION BY OBJECTIVES

Most practices in evaluating teachers are deficient. As mentioned in Chapter 1, more than one-half of the nation's teachers report no confidence in their school system's program of teacher evaluation. Student teachers are unhappy with the vague criteria for assessing their qualifications for entry into the profession. There is a way both to improve our procedures for identifying the unfit teacher and to improve the teaching competency of others. Execution of this plan—a behavioral model which has been labeled "supervision by objectives"—will at the same time increase the learning of pupils.

THE CONTRACT: AGREEMENT ON OBJECTIVES

Briefly, supervision by objectives is a process by which a supervisor and a teacher agree in advance on what they will accept as evidence that the teacher has or has not been successful in changing the skills, competencies, or attitudes of his students. The agreement is drawn up before the teacher acts and is designed to counter the prevailing practice of trying to make an *ex post facto* judgment of ends. The contract is tentative to the extent that at any time the parties can renegotiate. For example, the original target is modified if the teacher finds during the course of instruction that he has overestimated the changes possible or if he subsequently determines more important changes for his students. This will happen frequently and requires agreement from the supervisor that the modification is warranted and that the alternate criterion measures are acceptable.

The period of time during which the contract functions is variable. A contract can be used for guiding the observation of a single lesson, and in this case, the supervisor and teacher confer in advance as to what they will accept as an indication that pupils have learned from that particular lesson. A contract may also be written to cover a year's course of instruction. Evidence of effectiveness is then assessed at the end of the year with criteria agreed upon at the beginning of the year.

Learning theory and empirical data support the view that when there are clear statements of objectives learning is more efficient and objectives are attained more readily. Differences in objectives between supervisor and teacher are resolved *before* instruction under the contract plan, in contrast to those situations where teachers have been successful in producing changes in learners (have been successful teachers) but have failed on their ratings as teachers because the supervisor did not concur in the desirability of the results produced. The teacher and supervisor become partners in the enterprise. Advice and suggestions from the supervisor are then valued by the teacher, because they are related to the teacher's own desired changes in learners. When there is no agreement on goals, suggestions from supervisors tend to be viewed as irrelevant, as the supervisor's personal impositions upon the teacher.

BEHAVIORAL CHANGE AS EVIDENCE OF LEARNING

Basic to supervision by objectives are two assumptions. First, learning is evidenced by a change in behavior. For example, a child is given a problem such as $9 + \underline{\qquad} = 11$ and is asked to respond by completing the equation. If the child is unable to make the correct response, instruction follows; subsequently, the child is presented with the same problem or new instances of the class of problems involving the inverse relationships of addition and subtraction. If he is now able to make the correct response, we say he has learned, because learning is shown when one responds to particular situations or classes of situations in new ways. There is no way of knowing whether a change has occurred without observing a behavior or consequence of behavior, such as a product, composition, or other tangible work. Second, teaching is successful only when the instructor's predetermined and intentional change in the learner actually occurs. If the desired responses do not follow, teaching is ineffective.

The criterion problem in teacher evaluation arises because of differences in interpretation of ideals and because of the failure to distinguish means from ends. Historically, teaching encompasses more than the ability to produce a behavioral change. We speak of the importance of questioning techniques, of the value of a teacher whose voice is of high quality and whose conduct in the community is exemplary. The qualities associated with the good teacher are unlimited, and even when we agree upon the importance of certain ideals, we have not agreed on how these ideals shall be manifested in specific behavior. Is good citizenship best manifested by protest or conformity? Further, we have too frequently made the means of instruction the criterion rather than testing to see if the means really produce more important instructional outcomes. Following the behavioral model of supervision, there would be an attempt to secure initial agreement between the supervisor and teacher on specific changes to be wrought in learners, thereby clarifying the meaning of ideals and ensuring that the instructional intents are present to guide the selection of means. If there is no agreement on the ends of instruction, then there can be no meeting of minds regarding the appropriate procedures to follow in the classroom and no fair assessment of teacher effectiveness. A teacher cannot accept suggestions from a supervisor regarding teaching practice if that practice is inconsistent with the behavioral changes deliberately planned by that teacher. Many arguments as to whether or not a teacher is following sound principles of learning are actually arguments over differences in outcomes sought from instruction. There is, for instance, no particular value in the frequently recommended practice of pupil participation in classroom discussions if the objective is the ability to recall information from printed sources. In fact, silent reading of a textbook might be more appropriate for the latter objective because of its saving in time.

Supervision by objectives requires a shift from judging a teacher's competency by the procedures followed in the classroom to judgment in terms of the results the teacher is getting with learners. We are now saying that we do not know with certainty which methods will produce the desired results, but that we are willing to find out—the teacher is viewed as an inquirer or hypothesis-maker and tester and not one who has arrived in his craft. The principal of a school and a teacher must not regard an instructional practice (whether seats are in one direction; whether the teacher talks most, all, or some of the time) as an end in itself. The questions to be asked are: "How are these things related to the changes we are trying to effect in boys and girls?" "How will a specific procedure bring about the results we seek?" What the pupil is asked to do and know as a result of a single lesson, a semester, or a year's course of study can be specified. *We cannot teach what we cannot specify.*

INAPPROPRIATE AND LIMITED INSTRUMENTS OF EVALUATION

In those situations where teachers distrust evaluation, the most flagrant criticism of supervisors is that they observe a teacher's performance without knowing what the teacher is trying to accomplish. The principal who visits a room without knowing the objectives of the lesson is likely to attend to room environment, noticing, for example, the blinds aren't even, or to make some inane comment about the nice children. In a sense, judging the teacher independently from the consequences sought and attained is like judging a ball player on the basis of his form rather than observing where the ball goes. We sometimes even judge performance of the teacher without first finding out what game he is playing. If there is agreement initially by the supervisor and the teacher upon the desired ends of instruction—whether they be with respect to subject-matter attainment, changed attitudes toward civic problems, or the solution of the learner's personal problems—then the teacher has a chance to succeed and an opportunity to profit from supervisory assistance when the objectives are not being met.

Instruments for evaluation have fostered narrowness of instructional objectives and have served particular interests. What is important is what we look for in observation. Observation of instruction was formerly based heavily on the belief that the teacher should be an example of an ideal, and early instruments for guiding observations called attention to the personal qualities of the teacher, such as appearance, a factor that is still noted. In many student teaching assignments, novices frequently come close to tears because of personal criticism. Sometimes this unhappiness follows downgrading by the supervising teacher because of one's length of skirt, kind of eye makeup, and so on. The hair styles and clothes of male teachers also invite criticism. Emerson's comment is relevant here: "You are trying to make that man another you. One's enough."

Later a number of observational instruments were developed by people with particular axes to grind. Sociologists and mental hygienists provided a set of glasses for educators to use in viewing instruction, but they never made it clear that when one puts on these glasses, he automatically buys the objectives of the donor. For instance, there were observational schedules prepared by sociologists. What do sociologists view as the purpose of the school? Socialization of the child. What did they ask observers to look for? Peer group interactions. "Use your sociogram to find out who speaks to whom, under what conditions, and with what effect." "Who are the isolates and who are the stars?"

And what do mental hygienists conceive is the most important function of the school? Mental hygiene. As a consequence we have the study of Wickman, who asked psychologists to rate as most serious to least serious behavior like cheating, swearing, masturbating, remaining silent in the classroom (Wickman, 1928). The teachers were asked to list what they thought was the most serious behavior. Sure enough, teachers considered cheating and the like serious problems, but as for quiet in the classroom being a problem, teachers asked, "Are you kidding?" The psychologists went to work and established child study centers which taught teachers to identify the quiet child and regard him with suspicion. Subsequently, it was announced that teachers and psychologists were more nearly agreed in their views of serious behavior in terms of the framework—the framework of the psychologist.

Use of the analytical tools of specialized fields has a place, but schools have functions other than socialization and mental health—the acquisition of academic disciplines, problem-solving abilities, and cultural values. Therefore, we must have observation systems that are more value neutral and that will focus on variables relevant to the attainment of a range of objectives, not just the objectives of the sociologist and psychoanalyst.

Many educators have also developed observational instruments that reflect a particular value and bias. For instance, Marie Hughes looks at a teacher in terms of whether the teacher exercises a controlling, a content, or an encouraging function. It appears that encouraging behavior is prized most by Dr. Hughes (Hughes, 1959). If the teacher, therefore, has a different end, such as content mastery, he probably will be judged less favorably by users of the Hughes guidelines regardless of his success in obtaining content mastery among the pupils. Such situations illustrate the importance of agreeing on the ends first and then judging the effectiveness of the teaching.

OBSERVATION: COLLECTING FACTS
AND EVIDENCE

What should we look for when we observe? Let us remember that by our definition the good teacher is the one who is able to effect desired changes in the learner. Let us also admit that we don't have certain knowledge of how to produce these changes. There is no unequivocal interpretation of the desirability of any educational practice. That is why it is important to view each teaching situation as an experiment in which one says, "If I do these things, the learners will be able to make these responses," and to have the courage to see whether or not predicted results occur. When the desired consequences do not follow, one must attempt to reason why and try an altered approach, again noting consequences.

The observer of instruction must do two things: record factual descriptions of what took place during the lesson and collect evidence of the extent to which the desired results have occurred. Together, the facts noted during the lesson and the evidence of results can generate modified approaches or modified objectives. Among the kinds of incidents to be noted are opportunities to practice the desired behavior, the number of times each child had an opportunity to respond, and the confirmation or additional information given the learner following his responses. It is particularly important that the supervisor record actual events, not inferences. The supervisor can confront the teacher with a record of observable behavior; he cannot confront the teacher with inferences without facts to support them and expect anything except resistance. One might record that the redheaded boy continually hit his neighbor on the head with a pencil but should not merely record that the redheaded boy was not paying attention. The latter is an inference; the former is a fact. As an observer, I once wanted to say that a boy who hit another with a pencil was not paying attention, but my inference was wrong. The boy's subsequent responses to problems posed by the teacher showed he was "tuned in." I don't know about the boy he was hitting.

Social psychological variables and their indicators, such as the seating patterns of children and the frequency of correction given by the teacher, are useful analytical tools for guiding the observer; however, I repeat that the observed practice itself is to be tested. For example, we are told to look for instances of warmth in a teacher. There may be behavior that one could classify as warm and friendly, but warmth and friendliness as you define them might not be universal qualities to be sought in teachers. Warmth and friendliness are often in the eyes of the pupils rather than in the teacher or supervisor. It is difficult to find any teacher who is not seen as warm and friendly by at least one pupil and as cold by another. Teachers may be viewed by middle-class pupils as just or fair because these teachers keep their distance and show impartiality, but some children interpret this impartiality as coldness. By ways of example, there was a lad who was unhappy with his teachers until he met one many of us would classify as nagging and chastising. This boy responded by saying, "At last I've found a teacher who cares about me." A Mexican-American, the boy might have been responding to his cultural norm which says children should heed specific instructions from adults and not lead independent lives. I would be surprised, however, if pronouncing a learner's name correctly, consulting his interests, and interacting with his parents produced undesirable consequences. Nevertheless, we must regard our procedures as something to be tested and challenge our pet assumptions about what will work.

The behavioral model presented so far for the evaluation of instruction is narrow in that it focuses upon the teacher's ability to formulate and attain accepted educational objectives. In an attempt to control the particular bias of the supervisor or pressure groups, only those teaching practices which are found to be directly related to the attainment of the objectives are considered legitimate. As an instance of this bias, a novice teacher was subject to removal because she didn't put the paints back in the right place and was, therefore, labeled disorderly and unfit for teaching. We must distinguish judgments that rest upon professional knowledge from judgments that represent parochial preferences. If a community or board of education says it wants its teachers to be hard-shelled Baptists or Caucasians, these are parochial values not professional ones. The list of parochial expectations is unlimited. I am suggesting, however, that we give more attention to the professional qualifications of the teacher independent of parochial expectations and pressures. The professional supervisor must deal with the distinctive feature of teaching, the competency to select appropriate changes to be sought in learners and the ability to produce these changes. Our problem in supervision is to make explicit the behavioral changes we are attempting to effect in our learners. To the extent that there is agreement that these changes are desirable, we can plan effective programs and collect evidence that certain procedures are valid.

MODIFYING INSTRUCTIONAL PROCEDURES FOR BETTER RESULTS

Advocating that the teacher be judged by the changes produced in pupils is but half the solution to the problem, for if results are not favorable one must know how to modify instructional procedures. Impressions of teaching are not enough; factual observations are required to describe teaching. An analysis which will tell one what to vary in order to improve teaching effectiveness requires a description of the teaching act. What then shall be the basis for developing a framework for observation? So far we have indicated the existence of frameworks that are quite appropriate when the instructional outcomes are socialization, mental health, and objectives associated with progressive education in the 1940s. Our problem now is to develop analytical tools that can serve a wider range of instructional outcomes. Learning theory and principles offer wider generalization; theory is not tied to specific outcomes. The principle of overlearning, for instance, is held to increase retention of all behaviors, not just those associated with mental, physical, or moral considerations. However, the very fact that a principle of learning does not bear a one-to-one correspondence with a given classroom practice makes it difficult to agree whether or not the principle is being followed. For example, it is commonly accepted that one can modify the behavior of a learner by providing him with reinforcers or rewards following efforts which approximate the desired changes. But this principle requires specific agreement as to how the principle will be manifested in a given classroom before it is useful to supervisor and teacher. What will be accepted as evidence that reinforcement is present? Praise by the teacher? Special privileges? Opportunity to choose one's own task? Reinforcement, opportunity to practice the behavior desired, and knowledge of results are factors or principles which guide our observation, but they are not facts; they merely serve to elucidate the gathering of facts and the forming of generalizations from facts. Principles and theory are of little value in supervision unless they lead to analysis of data collected during the observation.

When trying to help a teacher improve, two requirements must be met. First, the teacher and supervisor agree on the objective(s) of the lesson and the kinds of evidence that will be collected indicating whether the objectives were reached or not. Second, the supervisor records descriptive facts (events that can be seen and heard) during the lesson. These facts can be selected and organized in terms of a principle of learning or other variable which one finds helpful in calling attention to factors that might otherwise be ignored. It must be emphasized, however, that the principle has no absolute validity; a principle is not a fact. A teacher becomes furious when a supervisor cannot give factual instances to back charges that the teacher did not follow principles of instruction, such as by failure to individualize.

Following the teaching and the collecting of evidence, the supervisor and teacher contrast intended outcomes with evidence of actual outcomes. Where insufficient progress is made by learners, supervisor and teacher together examine observations made during the lesson. Review of the facts and the casting of items in terms of an analytical framework may lead to suggestions to be tested in subsequent lessons. Observed lessons may reveal the need for more appropriate objectives as well as ways to vary practice.

SUMMARY

Thus far, a procedure for evaluating and improving instruction, called supervision by objectives, has been sketched. It places emphasis upon the consequences of instruction in terms of pupil gain, changes in attitude and self-concept as well as mastery of subject matter. The procedure does not throw out analytical schemes in the observation of instruction but relegates their use to guiding the supervisor in making a descriptive record and in analyzing this record. The point is stressed that principles of learning and instruction in the abstract are not sufficient, and that indicators of the presence or absence of these principles must be operationally defined. In this behavioral model, principle and theory are seen as sources for generating new approaches and modifications in teaching method. The model demands, however, that proposed departures be empirically tested, that evidence of the effect of the innovation be collected. The proposal is a timely one: the American public expects results from schooling. As the cost of public support increases, there will be increasing insistence on a factual basis for educational decisions. In the past, no one has taken such a basis very seriously, especially in making decisions regarding teacher effectiveness. The rising dissatisfaction of teachers regarding evaluation procedures is a case in point. If administrators and teachers are ready to negotiate on criteria for effectiveness that stress results in terms of desired behavioral changes in learners rather than to rely upon personal impressions of the teacher and his procedures as criteria for evaluation, we can avoid an educational scandal and at the same time improve the quality of learning for pupils.

chapter 4

FOUR PHASES
IN THE IMPROVEMENT
OF INSTRUCTION

Professor Robert H. Anderson at Harvard has pioneered in developing programs aimed at improving teaching. Those working under his leadership have employed a useful four-phase framework or cycle for organizing procedures in the supervising of teachers. Although there are differences of opinion about the procedures for use within each of these phases, there is general agreement on the value of differentiating stages in the supervisory act. Initial help in selecting instructional intents and role clarification of the observers occurs during phase one, the *preobservational conference*. The second phase is *observation*, which demands a recording of the teaching act. A third phase is termed *analysis and strategy*, a time devoted to interpreting the facts collected during observation and planning ways to share these interpretations with the teacher. The final phase is the *postobservational conference* where there is assessment by both teacher and supervisor of the results of the lesson and where use is made of the analysis in order to formulate subsequent teaching plans including new objectives and changed teaching strategies.

THE PREOBSERVATIONAL CONFERENCE

The preobservational conference between the teacher and those who will observe the lesson occurs at least one day in advance of the lesson to be taught. Because often the teacher will want to change objectives and teaching plans as a consequence of new insights gained from the meeting, the conference is not scheduled immediately before he is to teach. The conference is attended by the teacher and those who are going to observe the lesson or assess its effects, for example, master teacher, principal, consultant, or peer—all are supervisors when engaging in this cycle. A chief purpose of the conference is to ensure that all are agreed on the instructional intents of the teacher and on how evidence will be gathered to show that the intents are fulfilled, that is, what learners will be able to do after instruction that they could not do before, how this change will be manifested, to what degree the learner will acquire mastery of the task. Also, the teacher must specify whether he expects all pupils to reach this expectation, and if not, he should stipulate the modified standards to be exhibited by individuals.

When the purpose of supervision is to improve instruction and *not* simply to judge the competency of a teacher, the supervisor should define at the conference his forthcoming role as a fellow problem-solver, not rater, during observation analysis sessions. The teacher should know that the supervisor will focus on the extent to which the pupils attain the objective(s) set by the teacher and on describing the interactions between student and teacher that relate to the objective. Generally the supervisor will not observe the lesson from the point of view of other objectives which have not been agreed upon in advance, although in some situations the teacher may want the supervisor to observe learner's behavior without reference to the objective in order that new needs for the pupils can be established and new objectives formed. This special request, however, should be made and accepted at the preobservational conference.

It is much better if the teacher is assured that, when a supervisor observes for the purpose of improving instruction, the teacher is not to be punished if the pupils do not achieve as intended. When emphasizing improvement, immediate success with pupils is less important than helping the teacher (1) recognize that learners have not achieved and (2) acquire a willingness to look at the analysis of the lesson with the idea of planning new instructional strategies. Most lessons are not successful: effecting a change in a learner is difficult. We need teachers who, when confronted with evidence that learners are not progressing as desired, are able and willing to modify their teaching and, in turn, test these modifications. This is a far cry from the teacher who either does not check to see if learners attain objectives or when faced with poor results blames the learners and carries on in the same manner "only louder."

The following are characteristics of a "good" preobservational conference.

1. *Agreement as to what the teacher intends to achieve.* The intents are stated in terms of what pupils will be able to do that they could

not do at the start of the lesson. The supervisor and teacher may not always be in agreement that the objective selected is the best one to teach. When teachers are just starting to participate in preobservational conferences, they sometimes need assurance. They need to learn to trust the supervisor. By way of supervisory strategy, it is recommended that the supervisor focus first upon *instructional deficiencies* (helping teachers find new instructional procedures for the ends he has in mind) rather than focusing upon *curricular deficiencies* (trying to get the teacher to select ends of greater merit). The focus on curricular deficiencies can come in later sessions. With apprehensive teachers, the supervisor will promptly decide not to bear down hard in the first "preob" in getting the teachers to formulate objectives of greater worth. Instead, the supervisor will be interested in seeing how effective the teacher is in attaining an objective with which he feels most confident. On the other hand, teachers who have had two or more conferences should be challenged on their choice of objectives. The teacher should be asked to justify each objective in terms of its importance to anticipated instructional tasks, its relevance to the children at hand, its appropriateness to social conditions today and to those expected in the future, its factual correctness, and the like.

One of the chief values of the preobservational conference is that it helps teachers consider objectives which would otherwise be overlooked. The supervisor need not always know the most important objective which should be taught but should play a "devil's advocate" in getting the teacher to generate more appropriate objectives. The teacher who continues to state objectives which lack validity is a teacher who has a *curricular deficiency* signaling the need for preparation in a subject field and in curriculum development. After conducting a number of "preobs," the supervisor will be struck by the way teachers differ in their expectations as to what can be taught in, say, a 30-minute lesson. At first some teachers state objectives that would be more realistic in a ten-week period or a year's course of instruction. Others state objectives that are invalid because the pupils already possess the competence which the teacher is intending to teach. The latter error is more common, so common, in fact, that a rule should be established requiring the teacher to pre-assess pupils on the objective before the preobservational conference and arrive at the conference with evidence that the learners indeed have not already mastered the objective.

2. *Agreement on plans for collecting evidence that the learners have or have not reached the objective.* At the end of the conference, supervisors and teacher should know how the teacher will collect evidence that the learners have or have not achieved. Usually, this proposal for the collecting of evidence takes the form of giving a random sample of pupils (or the entire class) problems that they could not solve at the beginning and then seeing if they can solve them at the end of the lesson. Some objectives, such as those which call for the learner to display a particular *process* or way of working rather than just getting the "right" answer, require that three or four pupils be asked to attack a problem after instruction while the teacher and supervisor observe to see if the desired process is exhibited. Evidence that some objectives have been

reached can be found in the *product* which a learner can produce after instruction. Written compositions, for instance, can be examined to see if they subsequently have qualities such as multiple sentence patterns, colorful words (modifiers), and more accurate punctuation. Also, the teacher may elect to sample indicators of the *attitudes* of pupils to see if they are favorable to a newly introduced activity or learning experience. Simply asking the children to write a *yes* or *no* response anonymously to the question, "Would you like to do this again?" may give a clue as to whether pupils have positive feelings toward the activity.

Supervisors and teachers should be careful to note that the test or evidence sought matches the performance called for in the objective. To have an objective which states that learners will be able to properly construct something requires that the test demands that learners actually construct, not merely point to items that are and are not properly constructed. Also, just so there will be no argument after the lesson as to whether the teacher meant that all of the class or one-third of the class would reach the objective, the teacher and supervisor should agree in advance on the percentage of the class who will achieve the objective before the lesson will be considered successful.

3. *Agreement on the role the supervisor will play during observation.* The teacher should know that the supervisor is in the room during the lesson for the purpose of recording teacher-pupil interactions (such as questions and responses), the instructional stimuli presented, and what pupils do when given these stimuli.

At one time there was a rule that the observer should not make notes in the presence of the pupils and teachers. That rule might have been needed when the teacher did not know what kind of data was being gathered or what inferences the supervisor might be jotting down in order to later clobber the teacher. With supervision by objectives the teacher knows that the supervisor is recording those aspects of pupil-teacher exchange that can be seen and heard. He is not recording inferences or commenting about the teacher's appearance (unless such appearance might be a key problem in the attainment of the objective). The teacher must recognize that the more accurate the data collection, the better chance there will be to analyze the lesson and derive alternative approaches in the event the objective is not reached (that pupils do not change as intended by the teacher). Whether the supervisor is writing rapidly and continually to get the classroom dialog down or whether a videotape machine is doing the recording job, the teacher must accept that an analysis of the lesson requires data—observation of the teaching event—and that it is the supervisor's job to collect these data.

Occasionally a teacher will want the supervisor to make specific observations unrelated to the instructional objectives. The teacher may want the supervisor to focus on some aspect of the teacher's personal behavior in the classroom, such as what learners do when the teacher uses certain language in explanation. These special requests should be made at the time of the preobservational conference.

OBSERVATION

An observation should result in data, not just a generalization. The untrained observer confuses two tasks in supervision of instruction: (1) recording what the teacher and pupils do during the instructional session (data) and (2) generalizing the meaning of the actions seen and heard. Many currently used instruments and systems for the study of teacher behavior, such as the popular one promoted by Amidon and Flanders, demand that the observer not record the actual words and actions used by the teacher but make a tally or summary of events that fall within a category of teacher-pupil behavior (Amidon and Flanders, 1963). Differences between generalizations and actual data can be seen below:

Generalization or Category	*Data*
1. Teacher gives instruction.	"Circle the pictures of animals that are not warm-blooded."
2. Teacher rephrases pupil responses.	"Tom meant to say that *some* Scotchmen are tight."
3. Teacher lets a pupil know a response is correct.	"Very good. When you add the 4 it does make 12."

Note that the generalized statements are far less accurate. They are also less useful in helping a teacher see in detail what is happening during classroom interaction. As generalizations, they are economical in that one does not have to look at specific incidents in order to focus upon the teacher's characteristic style. However, the teacher can best accept these statements as generalizations when they are accompanied by the data from which they are drawn.

The usefulness of data cannot be overemphasized. To point out that the teacher spent one-third of a lesson in giving instruction may be of some importance, but critical analysis will not occur without opportunity to examine the nature of the instruction given. For instance, in the first illustration above, if pupils did not respond to instruction, the teacher and supervisor can use the data to hypothesize why. Did the children not know the meaning of "circle," or was it that they could not recognize positive instances of "warm-blooded?" See also how much more information is contained in the data column opposite number 2. It may be helpful for a teacher to know that he is continually rephrasing pupil responses, but it will be more valuable to know the nature of the rephrasing. Are the rephrased statements the kind that would diminish respect or the self-concept of the pupil? Actual data are necessary to make such inferences. Also, in example number 3 one can see that the data tell us the teacher is giving more than knowledge of correctness of response—he is giving words of praise.

Generalizing and analyzing should be separated from recording of data. Ideally an observer will record all instances of pupil-teacher interaction. A videotaped lesson is one form of such a record. A film which faithfully records verbal and visual responses of participants is a good observation, but many videotapes fail to focus on all pupils or representative samples of pupils. Most observations are in the form of notes, written protocols of verbal interactions between pupil and teacher. The records report what is said rather than what is seen, and there is less attention given to nonverbal behavior such as expressions on faces. Making of records of verbal behavior requires that the observer write fast, perhaps using a shorthand system, for example *c* for child. After the record is made, the specific responses should be then categorized, generalizations formed, and other interpretations of the data made. When one attempts to analyze and interpret while recording, he will miss valuable data and risk drawing inferences which are neither valid nor comprehensive. Also, if one looks only for data which might support a generalization in a single category of teacher behavior (the category which is serving as an advanced organizer), he is likely to have an invalid picture of that teacher's practices. For example, to concentrate on collecting data that can be categorized as indicators of "teacher use of criticism" is likely to be less valuable than collecting a wide range of data. Comprehensiveness of data allows interpretations about the teacher's habits of criticism as well as other practices which together give a more descriptive picture of that teacher's conduct.

Observation should be more descriptive than interpretive, providing descriptive facts with which the teacher can make interpretations and decisions regarding future practice. Choice of words used in the record can reveal whether one is describing or interpreting. To diagnose your own ability to differentiate statements of description from interpretations, try identifying the descriptive statements found in the list below:

1. The girl is stumbling into the room.
2. The girl has her hands on her face.
3. The teacher is chastizing the child.
4. The girl is ashamed of what she has done.
5. The boy does not like the lesson.
6. The boy is holding the microscope in his right hand.
7. The boy is confused by the explanation.
8. The teacher is talking too much.
9. The teacher has his back to the class.
10. The teacher asked 5 questions beginning with *what*, 1 question beginning with *how*, and none with *why*.

Numbers 2, 6, 9, 10 are descriptive.

Practical Answers to the Problem
of Too Much Data

Principals, fellow teachers, and others who should participate in observation and subsequent sessions of analysis often do not because they think it takes too much time. Furthermore, to reproduce in writing what happens during a 45-minute class period is tiring, and there is so much information collected during 45 minutes that one is overwhelmed with data and often despairs of making sense out of it.

The concept of *microteaching* offers a solution to the complexity of classroom observation. Microteaching is real teaching; it lessens the complexities of classroom teaching by reducing the class size, scope of content, and time; it allows the teaching to focus on the accomplishment of specific tasks; it permits one to reveal particular instructional skills and techniques of teaching. Through microteaching, teachers can show their own mastery in using certain curricular materials, or a microteaching lesson can be staged to provide evidence of how the teacher acts with given kinds of students and in the presence of other factors believed to influence one's teaching (Allen and Ryan, 1969). In microteaching, instead of teaching 45-minute lessons, the teacher is asked to select an objective which he thinks can be taught in 5 minutes. After observation, this 5-minute lesson becomes the basis for analysis. Recording of the lesson by observers occurs through videotape, tape recorder, or paper-and-pencil recording. In addition to limiting the lesson to approximately 5 minutes, the number of students involved can be reduced from, say, 30 to 5, and by focusing on the responses of 5 pupils, observers can be more reliable. When starting to learn how to make observations, it is often desirable to begin by observing lessons of short duration and few pupils. Subsequently, lessons can be of longer duration and pointed toward more advanced objectives, and the number of pupils to be taught can be increased, approximating the situation found in more normal classrooms. Some persons may be surprised at what learning can be accomplished in a 5-minute lesson. Insistence on a short microlesson is based on the demand for a highly focused, highly concentrated experience. Five minutes of teaching gives both teacher and observer plenty to consider. The short teaching experience, as opposed to longer sessions, allows for reliable recall of specific instances during the teaching episode and provides a manageable amount of data for practicing analysis of instruction.

Teams of observers offer another way for dealing with the embarrassment of too much teaching to observe. A team can be organized so that each member records only those instances which fall within a given category for which he is responsible, or each team member may monitor the responses of a few specific pupils. Possibilities exist for more sophistication in the staging or selection of lessons to be observed. The supervisor may want to see only lessons dealing with certain levels of objectives (one calling for the learners to recall information, one demanding that learners apply a concept to new situations). Or the teacher may want the observer to record what is happening during instruction to learners with given characteristics (the extremely anxious child, the child who will not compete, or the one who competes but doesn't cooperate). The team system can be economical of time and data-collecting by arranging teaching situations which promise to reveal particular teaching practices, practices which would not be present by chance.

Effects of Observers' Beliefs upon Observations

It is said that most observation systems are unreliable. Brown and Stoffell speculate that this is because the behavior of the teacher is unstable, because the recording practices of the observers are inconsistent, or because observers are unable to agree on what occurs (Brown and Stoffell, 1968). My own view is that the problem lies in confusing interpretation with description. What is called an observation system turns out to be an interpretation of what is going on, not a factual recording of what can be seen or heard. Let me admit, however, that the decision to select certain facts and ignore others will result in factual recording without meeting the criterion of objectivity. For this reason, I argue that it is usually better to record all verbal behavior during the lesson. Brown and Stoffell say their discoveries support the thesis that beliefs of observers influence observation of teachers' classroom behavior. This conclusion rests on their finding that groups of observers who are experimentalists in their educational philosophies and groups of observers who are opposed to John Dewey's philosophy of experimentalism differ in what they "see" when viewing teaching practices. The observers who are experimentalists see relatively fewer experimental teaching practices than do those whose own belief orientation is nonexperimental. It is speculated that experimentalists are looking at less experimentation than they would like to see and that both groups of observers tend to exaggerate those practices to which they are opposed. "Negative" or "bad" practices are the ones which they notice, just as the automobile driver pays most attention to other drivers on the road whose driving practices irritate him, while virtually ignoring those drivers who please him by meeting his expectations. Or, it may be that expertise is operating. Observers who are in high agreement with Dewey's experimentation are likely to know more about it. Their sensitivity to the concept tends to make them hypercritical of teachers who fail to come up to their high expectations with respect to experimentation, and they tend to be stingy in recording experimental practice. Something like two observers of opera—one who hates opera and knows little about it and one who likes and knows a great deal about it. Both are asked to record specific behavior on the opera stage. The opera lover is likely to be more precise and more demanding in his analysis of the performance than is the opera hater. Even though the whole thing may sound like uncontrolled screeching and screaming to the opera hater, he is likely to respond more kindly to a mediocre performance than is his expert colleague, because he cannot distinguish good opera from bad opera by any standard. Notice that Brown and Stoffell are talking about analysis and judgment as observations. My point is that the judging and analyzing of lessons should follow observation and not necessarily be done simultaneously with observation. Objectivity in observation comes with the recording of concrete, specific behaviors, and the more complete the record, the more objective it will be.

ANALYSIS AND STRATEGY

In the analysis session, one first looks at the results (were the objectives attained as desired?). If the answer is *no*, then the analysis should throw light on why this might be so, suggesting new teaching procedures to try and to test, new objectives to reach. If the answer is *yes*, then the analysis might indicate what made the lesson successful as well as point to the direction for subsequent lessons.

Analysis is not teaching but reflection upon the teaching act. An analysis may be as simple as noting whether or not the teacher was standing before a visual display, thereby making it impossible for the pupils to get information necessary for learning. It can also be as complex as applying an analytical scheme requiring special training before use, for example, the techniques for analyses developed by Amidon and Flanders (1963), Bellack (1969), and Medley (1963).

More than 75 systems exist for classifying classroom interaction, many of which are modifications of Flanders' way to record and classify verbal statements made in the classroom. Such systems give information such as (1) who talks and how much, (2) extent of group participation, (3) the emotional climate of the classroom, (4) the kind of thinking that is most evident, and (5) changes in verbal behavior under different circumstances.

The danger in using these systems is that one begins to believe that the presence or absence of a statement in certain of the categories called for is automatically good or bad. When one quantifies the amount of teacher talk to pupil talk in a lesson, he tends to assume that the teacher who talks most of the time is doing something wrong. Actually the proper ratio of teacher to pupil talk is relative to a particular objective and to given learners. There are times when a teacher should talk all of the time, other times when he shouldn't talk at all. Similar conclusions could be drawn for more than a hundred teacher behaviors used in analyzing a lesson. Quantification showing amount of student-initiated questions, teacher use of statements that include judgment rather than fact, teacher's rejection of pupil factual answers or teacher disapproval of pupil interpretation, and so on, should be tested, not prized or abhorred as teaching practices of inherent worth or harm.

Place of Theory in Analyzing Lessons

Man continues to develop his theoretical models for indicating how he thinks teaching should proceed. The task of those engaging in classroom problem solving is not to laugh at nor blindly accept these models but to test them and to use them in drawing attention to factors that are present but which they would not otherwise see. These factors may or may not influence pupil gain. Gagné, for instance, has introduced a model in which he specifies eight kinds of learning (Gagné, 1970). One kind, signal learning, is very simple: the individual learns to make a general response to a signal. Another is multiple discrimination learning, in which the individual learns to make different responses to many different stimuli that resemble each other in physical appearance. Other kinds are termed concept learning, principle learning, and problem solving. It is Gagné's belief that lower kinds of learning in a given field (mathematics, science, language, reading) must be mastered before the higher kinds can be learned. It may be that by gaining skill in the use of Gagné's model one can identify sequential patterns in the presentations of instruction by a teacher which might be reordered to good effect. Because we do not have principles of teaching which are valid in all situations, we cannot with certainty tell a teacher what he should do in a classroom in order to get results. Why then analyze? We analyze to select factors which may help us design new teaching procedures in hope that these new procedures will bring better results. In trying innovative practices in which we manipulate the factors, we validate the practices and show the power of the variable by noting what happens to pupils, not by assuming that the procedures are better because someone in authority says they are better. One should not accept a procedure simply because someone or some theory holds that the new procedure will work better than a current practice.

True, there are some factors which promise to be more useful in the design of instruction than others. Hilgard has summarized psychological "principles" of potential use in practice (Hilgard, 1967). However, as seen in the examples below, these principles are general statements which do not give sufficient specific direction to a teacher but only indicate a point of departure in analyzing and planning lessons:

1. Repetitive practice is important in learning a skill.
2. Positive rewards and success aid learning.
3. The learner should be active. He should make the responses we want him to learn.
4. It is important to practice a new learning in varied contexts if the teacher expects it to generalize.
5. A learning problem should be presented so that essential features (interrelating parts) are open to inspection by the learner.
6. Goal setting by the learner is important as motivation.
7. Divergent thinking (inventive solutions, creation of novel products) should be nurtured along with convergent thinking (logically correct answers).
8. With some tasks high anxiety learners perform better if *not* reminded of how well or poorly they are doing; low anxiety learners do better if they *are* interrupted with comments on their progress.
9. The group atmosphere of learning (competition versus cooperation; isolation versus group work) will affect satisfaction in learning as well as the products of learning.

10. Some long-range goals affect short-range activities. Thus college students of equal ability may do better in courses perceived as relevant to their majors than in those perceived as irrelevant.

Eclectic Use of Tools

Teachers and supervisors should be eclectic in their use of tools for analyzing instruction, not wed to a single theoretical model. In the absence of a single scheme of instruction that can "work" for the teacher in getting results, it is better to try and test a host of plausible ideas from a variety of sources—experienced teachers, behavioral scientists, psychologists, sociologists, etc. An example of eclectic ideas which may be useful in analyzing lessons appears in Figure 3.

The difficulty of finding any single instructional variable that alone contributes to achievement of pupils is shown in a study by Rosenshine. This investigator checked out the association between (1) teachers who were successful and teachers who were unsuccessful in teaching two 15-minute lessons prepared from identical material and (2) variables developed from research in linguistics and instructional set, experimental studies of instruction, and multivariate studies of the behavioral correlates of teaching effectiveness (142 variables). Only three of these variables reliably discriminated between teachers whose pupils made high and low scores on the common posttest (Rosenshine, 1968). The three significant practices were:

1. Rule and example-rule pattern of discourse. Teacher used a pattern of explanation which opens with a structuring statement, follows it with details, and concludes by restating the statement.

Figure 3 FACTORS THAT MAY BE USEFUL
IN ANALYZING INSTRUCTION

Presentational Factors	*Kinds of Data*
Pupils able to succeed (difficulty of lessons and concept of mastery)	Illustrations from the lesson that pupils cannot respond correctly, can respond correctly (error rate).
Opportunity to practice objectives	Describe incidents where pupil has opportunity to practice a task identical to that called for in the objective.
Level 1	Describe incidents where pupils are asked to solve problems identical to one given by teacher in his explanation.
Level 2	Describe incidents where pupils are asked to solve new problems of the same class of problems with which the lesson deals.
Knowledge of results	Incident and number of times teacher gives:
	1. indication of correctness or incorrectness of pupil responses
	2. information as to what it takes to have a correct response
Prompting	1. Incidents and number of times questions are rephrased when pupils do not respond appropriately.
	2. Incident and number of times teacher gives hint as

Figure 3 (continued)

	to the correct answer or number of examples.
	3. Incident and number of times teacher gives review questions.
Pacing	Record number of new concepts or skills introduced in session.
	Record number of pupils who are able to finish tasks given. Record latency of pupils' responses.
Ratio pupil-teacher talk	Each three seconds observe (record) whether pupil or teacher is talking—later compute the ratio.
Ratio pupil-teacher initiated questions	Number of times pupil initiated the contact; number of times teacher solicited the contact.
Preassessment	Number of pupils who do not already possess stated objectives as indicated by pretext or other evidence.
Perceived purpose	Evidence that pupils can state reasons for the learning task. Evidence that pupils can give examples of what they will be able to do at the end of the lesson.
Rule and example pattern	Record incidents when teacher did and did not state principle to be learned, gave examples

Figure 3 (continued)

	of principle and restated the principle.
One-sided vs. two-sided argument	Record teacher's arguments in discussing an issue.
Embellishment, for example, humor	Describe instances of embellishment.
Teacher's Personal Factors	
Nonverbal affect, for example, touching pupil	Describe.
Movement and gesture	Describe.
Reference to students' interest outside of class	Record what teacher said.
Number of alternative activities available, such as cooperative and competitive games; pupils free to select own activities	Describe.
Teacher expansion of student ideas	Give examples.
Ratio of praise to criticism (but be careful —how do you know it was seen as praise—you must have data of what teacher did or said and observation of pupils' response)	
Linguistic Factors	Evidence from teacher's statements.
Length of words used	

Figure 3 (continued)

Prepositional phrases
used

Use of personal
references, such as "I"

Use of negative
statement, such as
something that is not

Use of explaining links,
such as "because, if-then,
consequently"

---

2. Explaining links. Teacher explained frequently by using prepositions and conjunctions which indicate the cause, result, means, or purpose of an event or idea. Words and phrases such as "because," "in order to," "if . . . then," "therefore," and "consequently." The effective teachers used more of these words per lecture, per minute, and per 100 words.
3. Gesture and movement. Gesture was defined as movement of the arms, head, or trunk, and movement was movement from one fixed place to another.

If observation shows that a teacher is not getting results desired and is not using any of the three practices above, it might be worthwhile to see if learners start to achieve more after the teacher tries giving explaining links, using more rule-example patterns, and displaying gesture and movement.

Variables Useful in Analyses

When the purpose of analyses is to derive new objectives and new teaching strategies, some instructional principles have been found useful because they apply to the teaching of many different objectives and many kinds of pupils. These principles can be easily acquired, and their application will reveal possibilities for changing one's sequences of instruction as well as one's instructional objectives.

Appropriate Practice Supervisors should look at the data to see if the pupils had opportunity to practice the kind of behavior implied by the objective. If a teacher of mathematics, for instance, wanted the pupils to be able to solve word problems, did pupils practice with word problems and not engage in continuous practice on equations alone?

Knowledge of Results The learner should be given an indication of whether his responses are correct. Does the data show that there was "feedback" to tell the learner whether he was on the right or wrong track? Was the pupil given a clue to what his efforts were producing in order to increase the likelihood of improvement?

Identifying Prerequisites We assume there are some subject matters that are best learned when presented in a hierarchical order, for example, when during a lesson on multiplication, there is evidence that learner(s) cannot add, it makes sense to suggest that the teacher formulate and teach to a new objective in addition before directly pursuing the problem of teaching multiplication. Another assumption is that learners find participation in a learning task rewarding when that task is itself rewarding or is associated with an activity or with someone by whom the learner has been rewarded in the past. When data from an observation indicate that learners are "turned off" by an instructional activity (regard it as an aversive stimulus), it may be helpful to get information on what the learners have found previously rewarding and use this as a means to equip the learner with a more favorable attitude or predisposition, as a prerequisite to the task at hand.

Strategy for Planning the Postobservational Conference

When planning strategies for dealing with a teacher, a team of supervisors already know the discrepancy between what the teacher stated pupils should achieve (original instructional intents) and what pupils actually achieved. Supervisors also have a record of what pupils and teacher said and did during instruction. Data in these records have been looked at from a variety of ways ——the extent to which learners had a chance to practice the behavior called for in the objectives, what the teacher did when pupils evidenced confusion and error, indications of harmful rivalry between classmates, and so on. As a consequence of these analyses, some new objectives might be warranted. Also, the analyses will probably suggest changes in teaching procedure that promise to produce better results.

Questions of strategy include: Will we share the data and analyses with the teacher by letting him draw his own implications and formulate for himself new objectives and procedures? Do we want the teacher to provide any data that we might not have or to tell us his own feelings about the lesson? Why?

Are we going to follow the old-time admonition "tell him something nice about his teaching and then let him have it"? If we are trying to avoid giving personal judgment of the teaching and prefer to let results in terms of pupil progress determine "goodness" and "badness," do we neither praise or condemn what we saw? How much of the analysis should be shared in the first conference? Is it better to select one aspect of the instruction and do a thorough job? Can we treat several observed factors without overwhelming the teacher, making it difficult for him to reflect and act upon the content presented? What part of our analysis points to a *curricular* problem—inappropriate objectives? What part has implications for *instructional* improvement—new teaching procedures? Are we all agreed that no one will make any comment about the teaching without having data available to back up the statement?

How can we be sure that the teacher hears the information we believe important for him to have? Will we assign responsibility to each person to share particular information with the teacher? Is there anyone on the supervisory team who is reluctant to share information with the teacher even if it is based on facts because he fears it will make the teacher angry? Do we believe that a teacher knows when a group of supervisors is not "leveling" with him? If a teacher has his own evidence that a lesson was not successful, will he not lose confidence in those who pretend that all was "rosy cozy"?

POSTOBSERVATIONAL CONFERENCE

Evidence that a good postobservational conference has occurred is seen when the teacher leaves the conference with new objectives he wants to try to achieve, new instructional procedures to try out, and plans for checking the results that follow implementation of the new departures.

During the course of the conference, the teacher

should be given opportunities to hear the point of view of others about the teaching act under discussion. However, these opinions will not reflect the personal outlook of the supervisor independent of concrete observations. The theory expressed will be a response to the data, data from which the teacher and other supervisors may derive different interpretations. The validity of the points of view will be tested in the classroom as the teacher agrees to follow suggestions and to note the effects of these suggestions when acted upon with pupils.

The following is a brief summary of some of the chief characteristics found in the four stages:

Preobservation Phase
1. Evidence is presented from preassessment that learners cannot perform the task.
2. Relation of objective to long-term objectives, to learner, to other factors is given.
3. The objective is clarified, and a way to measure change in learner is proposed. There is agreement on the teacher's criterion of success.
4. Team members clarify what their future roles will be during observation, analysis, and post-observational conferences.

Observation Phase
1. Data are collected. There is more stress on recording what can be seen and heard than upon making a judgment.
2. There is focus on learner responses and actions initiated by learners. Attention is given to describing presentational variables, such as questions posed by teacher.
3. Evidence of changes in learners (as agreed upon in the preobservational conference) is collected.

Analysis and Strategy

1. Results of the lesson are compared with previously stated desired results.
2. The lesson is analyzed. A number of instructional factors and principles are considered, such as the principle of appropriate practice.
3. Generalizations are formed from supporting data (no generalization is permitted without data to back it up).
4. A plan for conducting the postobservational conference is formed—for example, responsibility is given to team members for sharing data and inferences with the teacher; attention is given to the teacher's own expectations from the team; allowance is made for the teacher's own analysis of the lesson.

Postobservational Conference

1. The focus is on results attained versus results desired.
2. New objectives are derived from results, data, and inferences made during observation.
3. New teaching strategies (hypotheses) are considered.
4. The teacher indicates what strategies will be acted upon and validated in subsequent lessons.

chapter 5

TECHNICAL QUALIFICATIONS
FOR THOSE PARTICIPATING
IN THE IMPROVEMENT
OF INSTRUCTION

There are persons who, because of official positions such as principal or training teacher, hold a legal right to engage in the practice of supervising instruction. As in many fields, teaching also has its common garden variety of sideline quarterbacks who comment freely about what they think of another's teaching. These comments are usually made behind the back of the teacher concerned and are seldom beneficial. Destructive gossip and harmful classroom visits can be minimized by a formal program of teacher assessment and improvement, but participants in such a program—principal, department chairmen, teachers, parents—must first possess a number of technical skills and abilities. Four of these skills and abilities are of great importance and require special attention, because they are not acquired in general education:

1. Anyone planning to work with a teacher in instructional improvement should be able to construct a behavioral objective. This objective should display the four characteristics of behavioral objectives:
   a. Tell who is to exhibit the behavior to the learner, not the teacher.
   b. Identify the behavior to be exhibited.
   c. Identify the standard of performance (criteria).
   d. Identify the givens, restriction, or both.
2. Given an instructional objective(s), anyone who is competent in pedagogy should be able to describe what and how evidence will be collected to indicate that the objective has been reached. This description will call for evidence that is consistent with the objective and will utilize procedures that are economical of time. Inasmuch as this data is for the purpose of assessing instructional effectiveness (not diagnosis of individual learners), a sampling procedure should be used.
3. Given his own instructional objectives, a student of the teaching act should be able to state at least one objective (subobjective or en route objective) which is a prerequisite. He also should be able to state at least one objective, of longer range than the original objective, which is a "next step" in a hierarchical series of objectives. The linkage (relation) of prerequisite objectives, original objectives, and longer-range objectives should be evident.
4. Given a filmed episode of teaching, a short live demonstration of teaching, or a written description of a teaching act, a participant should be able to:
   a. Differentiate inferences from observations.
   b. Identify procedures that are and are not

consistent with the principle of appropriate practice.

SPECIFYING OBJECTIVES

We have said that one cannot teach what he cannot specify. A prerequisite for the specification of objectives is the ability to differentiate between an instructional activity and an operational objective. Test yourself to see if you have this prerequisite by completing the exercise below:

Test of Ability to Distinguish Activities from Instructional Objectives

Place an X before those items that are well-stated instructional objectives as opposed to activities.

1.____The learner will be able to react to impressions of pictures, music, and poetry that satisfy aesthetic needs.
2.____Given a number of written statements, the learner will be able to evaluate them.
3.____The learner will be able to indicate in writing whether specific pictorial instances are or are not examples of condensation.
4.____The learner will enjoy biography as well as fiction.
5.____Given two of the best known plays of Shakespeare, the learner will become familiar with them.
6.____The learner will reveal in writing that he comprehends the meaning of the Bill of Rights.

7._____Given a series of paragraphs, the learner will be able to distinguish those which are factual from those which present a slanted point of view.

8._____The learner will be able to write an essay which exemplifies a technique of imagery.

9._____Learners will be given the opportunity to discover that books can help in solving problems.

10._____The learner will be introduced to a number of educational experiences which feature "live" performances of orchestral instruments. His experience will include the use of pictures, recordings, exhibits, of orchestral instruments, and a visit to an orchestral rehearsal.

11._____When presented with incidents involving humor and nonhumor, the learners will be able to tell whether the incident is humorous or not. Humor will be defined as incongruity (something novel in a familiar setting), absurdity, impossibility, or a play on words (including double meaning).

12._____When confronted with problems involving degrees of longitude and latitude, the learner will be able to calculate distances.

13._____Learners will experiment with techniques of dry brush, stippling, blending, and overpainting. They will also be shown ways of painting with brush, sponge, or brayer.

14._____The teacher will explain to learners the different places in which one must use capital letters in a paragraph.

15._____During the lesson, the learner will be given opportunities to learn selected rules for prevention and control of disease. Among the rules are: those that show the importance of keeping pencils and fingers out of the mouth, using a handkerchief or tissue to cover coughs and sneezes, and avoiding handling an unfamiliar substance (for example, medicine).

16.____Learners will receive instruction in the techniques for recognizing differences in effect between poems that contain long vowel sounds and those with short vowel sounds.

17.____Learners will receive individual instruction by composing a paragraph of their own choice that includes a topic sentence, a unit of organization, and a conclusion.

Objectives are found in statements 3, 7, 8, 11, 12 above. If you were incorrect in your answers, it is probably because you did not apply these two keys: (1) Is there a situation, a given? For example—given a newspaper, a slide in the playground, a direction to open his book—for what kind of situation are we taking responsibility for preparing the learner? Sometimes the given is implied, for example, when it is said that the learner will be able to write an essay using a technique of imagery, the implication is that there will be an occasion for writing such an essay. (2) Is there an observable response that the learner should make in the presence of the situation? For example, should he be able to underline statements of fact as opposed to statements of opinion, go down the slide feet first, open his book. Look at the statements below and identify the statement which has both a situation and an observable response on the part of the pupil.

1. Pupils will read poetic protests against social conditions, using materials such as "The Man with the Hoe" by Markham and "Factory Children" by E. Browning.

2. Given two poems of poetic protest, pupils will state what the protests were about and identify the techniques used by the poet in arousing emotions.

Statement 2 has a situation and an observable pupil response. Note that an objective does not concern itself with *how* something is to be taught, it indicates what the learner will be able to do *after* instruction is terminated.

An objective starts with a conception of the end, not the beginning; an activity offers the possibility of teaching almost an unlimited number of different kinds of objectives. Statement 1 above, for instance, might result in learners being able to recognize instances of figurative language or to compose poems with alliteration. It might lead to pupils' being able to differentiate the poetry of Markham from the poetry of Browning, or it might mean that learners could compare what an older generation protested with the themes which the modern generation has taken as causes for social protest. The student of teaching should be able to tell which words depict observable behavior (that which can be seen and heard) as opposed to behavior which must be inferred. To label, to underline, to pronounce, to construct are examples of observable behavior. To comprehend, to understand, to appreciate must be inferred from some observable behavior on the part of the learner.

Look at the statements below and see if the two elements—situation and learner behavioral response—are present in either or both.

1. Given any letter, the learner can say its name.
2. Given the letter *a*, the learner can say its name.

Both 1 and 2 have the essential elements of an objective. The situation in the first statement is that the learner can be presented any letter, whereas in the second he can be presented the printed letter a. The respective responses sought are saying the names of all letters and saying the name of the letter a. These examples illustrate how an objective can be made more "powerful" or generalizable. When a situation refers to a class rather than to a specific event, it is more powerful. When a situation implies a large population of instances, it is more generalizable than when the situation is a population of one concrete person or event. It might be that a kindergarten teacher would have 2 as an objective for a single day early in the term; and 1 as an objective for a two-week period of instruction.

One should feel free to use more than one sentence in making clear what the objective is, and if it is likely that not everyone will have the same meaning for a key term in the objective, that term should be defined. For example, in the pretest on page 73, item 11 called for learners to identify instances of humor. Not everyone agrees on what constitutes humor. Therefore, additional arbitrary specifications are made—for example, the presence of humor would be manifested when the writing shows a play on words. If necessary one could, or course, define by example what is meant by such expressions as "play on words"—"Have you taken a bath? why? Is there one missing?"

Unless stated otherwise, a statement of instructional objectives means that the learner shall be able to perform as stated in all instances, that is, display perfect performance. If the teacher does not intend this, then another sentence or two should be added to the objective indicating what standard of performance on the part of the learner will be acceptable. Will the teacher be satisfied if the learner performs as stated one-third of the time, two-thirds of the time? Standards may increase with subsequent lessons. In teaching children to add any set of two-digit numbers, the teacher first may be satisfied with

80 percent accuracy; subsequently only 100 percent accuracy will suffice.

A caution should be expressed: correctly stating instructional objectives does not mean that the objectives are valid. That the objectives are desired by the teacher does not necessarily mean that they are desirable, nor that they have been proven to be important to attainment of other values. However, by stating instructional objectives that have the qualities of observable learner response, identification of the given, and a standard of performance, one will have a better chance of recognizing the validity or invalidity of the objectives.

Popham has said explicit objectives make it easier for educators to attend to important outcomes (Popham, 1969). To illustrate, if you were to ask a social science teacher what his objectives were for his government class and he responded as follows, "I want to make my students better citizens so that they can function effectively in our nation's dynamic society," you would probably find little reason to fault him. His objective sounds so professional and eminently worthwhile that few could criticize it; yet beneath such facades of profundity, many teachers are really aiming at extremely trivial kinds of pupil behavior changes. How often, for example, do we find "good citizenship" measured by a trifling true-false test? Now if we'd asked for the teacher's objectives in operational terms and had discovered that, indeed, all the teacher was attempting to do was promote the learner's achievement on a true-false test, we might have rejected the aim as unimportant (and have helped the teacher find more appropriate objectives). But this is possible *only* with the precision of explicitly stated goals.

Mager's booklet, *Preparing Instructional Objectives*, is a most useful introduction to writing of objectives (Mager, 1962). Besides using Mager's book, a supervisor can help teachers arrive at operational statements more rapidly by asking them to explain what it is that they do in their courses. From the teacher's description the supervisor can infer what he thinks a pupil could perform after such a course and share this inference with the teacher. The teacher can then react positively or negatively until the actual objectives are stated. One can look at sample test items with the teacher and from these items infer an objective. Another way to help a teacher state an objective is to let the teacher first state the objective in general and vague language, such as "the pupil will learn the main ideas in paragraphs." By questioning and asking the teacher to be more precise, this statement can be modified to meet the qualities of a properly stated objective: "Given paragraphs composed of factual writing, the learner will be able to differentiate sentences which are generalizations and sentences which support the generalizations."

The Center for the Study of Evaluation at U.C.L.A. has a project entitled the Instructional Objective Exchange, created to serve as a clearinghouse through which the nation's schools can exchange instructional objectives, thereby capitalizing on the developmental efforts of others rather than being obliged to commence afresh. The project has also developed measuring techniques suitable for assessing the attainment of the objectives available. This exchange allows teachers to select, if not formulate objectives; it is one answer to the charge that busy teachers do not have the time to generate their own objectives.

OVERCOMING CURRICULAR DEFICIENCIES

When working with a teacher on the quality of objectives selected, one can note how many of the objectives are at a relatively simple level and how many are at a complex level. The teacher should respond to such questions as: Are the interests of learners best served when all objectives are at a recall level and none demand application of some principle? Is a better curriculum one in which there are objectives furthering divergent as well as convergent responses in the learner? The taxonomies of educational objectives are tools that can be used for analyzing levels of objectives (Bloom, 1956; Krathwohl, 1964). An example of a simple aid for categorizing the behaviors called for in objectives appears below:

1. *Recognition*—to identify the correct alternative among a number of alternatives.
2. *Recall*—to retrieve information from memory.
3. *Translate*—to transfer given information into a new code (paraphrase).
4. *Infer*—to derive meaning that transcends literal meaning, to arrive at new conclusions beyond the surface facts and relations which are given.
5. *Create*—to produce a work of thought or imagination (requires a definition of what constitutes "thought" or "imagination").

Evidence that a teacher does not possess valid teaching intents indicates a *curricular deficiency*, that is, that he lacks knowledge of the process for determining *what* to teach (in contrast to the process of determining *how* to teach). A description of a process of curricular development by which teachers can formulate more appropriate goals for pupils is found in a monograph by Ralph Tyler (1965). The Tyler work is a good source for supervisors and teachers who wish to generate objectives which are now not recognized (do not exist) but a less useful tool for those who have permanently settled on *what* should be taught. Essentially Tyler recommends that data be collected describing (1) many aspects of society, (2) the status of subject-matter knowledge (essential methods, principles and concepts), and (3) the psychological needs of man. Implications of these data for instruction are then drawn, serving as the basis for formulating instructional objectives. Before the objectives are to be accepted, however, Tyler suggests that they be subjected to both a psychological and a philosophical screen. The psychological screen consists of knowledge from psychology which leads one to infer that a given objective has a high probability of being attained under classroom conditions which can be arranged. The philosophical screen consists of a number of questions such as: Should the school prepare one for life as it is or life as it should be? Ideally, objectives should be subjected to both screens.

Some curricular deficiencies can only be overcome by helping the teacher acquire new subject-matter knowledge. It can be argued that one will not teach essentials of a field when he himself cannot identify these essentials and probably cannot teach others to perform operations when he (the teacher) cannot demonstrate the desired performance. A teacher whose objectives in mathematics stress rote memorization and exclude processes of logic is probably deficient in mathematics.

A very practical technique for generating "better" objectives in the classroom is associated with observing and analyzing lessons. This technique makes use of two kinds of observations: observing behavior directly related to a teacher's prestated instructional intents and observing events which lead to new intents quite different in nature from the teacher's immediate task at hand. The first leads to the identification of *en route objectives* (objectives consistent with the original direction); the second frequently gives rise to an objective that may replace the original intent itself. To illustrate an en route objective, imagine a teacher who wants children to tell time to the nearest minute—(original objective: given a clock with hands at different positions, learner will state the hour and minutes). During the lesson it is observed (surprise) that some children cannot count to 12, some cannot count to 60; consequently, the teacher may establish a number of en route objectives for these learners who lack the prerequisite skills—for example, given a clock children will be able to count the numerals in a clockwise direction from 1 to 12. The teacher has not departed from the original objective, but he will not give more practice in trying to tell time without first making sure that learners acquire the en route objectives. In short, the teacher begins to teach specific objectives which were not originally contemplated.

As an illustration of formulating an objective in a direction different from an original objective, consider the case of a kindergarten teacher who had for her objective that given scissors, paper, and instructions to cut open along various kinds of folds, learners would be able to do so without departing from the edge of the fold. Now during the operation let us assume that some children are pointing their scissors at the faces of others and running with scissors in their hands. This observation could lead to the implication that children's following of safety procedures for use with sharp instruments should be an objective of higher priority than motor dexterity in cutting.

The conclusion to be drawn from these examples is that an objective for a lesson need not be considered of ultimate or absolute value. If a lesson results in the selection of a more important objective than the one with which instruction began, then from a curricular point of view that lesson has been successful. Dewey put it very well: "There is no such thing as a final set of objectives, even for the time being or temporarily. Each day of teaching ought to enable a teacher to revise and better in some respect the objectives arrived at in previous work" (Dewey 1929).

COLLECTING EVIDENCE OF CHANGE

Evidence is more than performance on paper-and-pencil tests. Objectives can be classified as emphasizing (1) *process*—the learner is to display the ability to go about resolving a problem in a given manner; (2) *product*—the learner must show that he can make a product which has certain specified qualities; (3) *solution to a cognitive task*—there is a problem or a class of problems posed, and the learner must demonstrate that he can solve the problem, which will involve mastery of an intellectual operation; or (4) *attitude*—the learner's predispositions are to be noted, showing responses toward something, someone, or self. Measurement of the ability to solve a cognitive task usually occurs by giving the learner a paper-and-pencil test (multiple-choice, completion, or problems to be solved), and this kind of measurement is so common that teachers do not always think about collecting evidence in other ways. The ease of measuring by paper-and-pencil tests probably leads to the selection of objectives which call for solutions to chiefly cognitive tasks.

Evidences of change in attitude, of acquisition of process and of capacities to produce products are often best indicated in ways other than pencil-and-paper tests. An indication of whether a learner's attitude toward certain types of literature or drama has changed can be found in a self-report, a log, a diary, an autobiography, some means by which the individual records what he is reading or viewing. Setting up situations outside the classroom and then noting how the learner acts in these situations and how he feels about them is another way to collect evidence regarding his predispositions to given situations.

Evidence of ability to employ a given process can be collected by placing the learner in a situation which calls for use of the process and then observing whether the learner follows the process or not as he proceeds. A checklist may help to record the steps followed, and noting changes in products produced (changes in the qualities of paintings, compositions, and such) is also easier and more accurate when one has a checklist of factors to observe when looking at the product.

Teachers should be encouraged to collect the evidence that best matches the objective they want to teach. They should not feel that since paper-and-pencil tests are easy to come by, objectives should be limited to performance on these tests. Examples of sources suggesting both ordinary and less common measures are available in such publications as those by Buros (1965) and Oppenheim (1966), and in the work of the Center for Evaluation at U.C.L.A. Buros' *Mental Measurement Yearbook* contains a listing and critique of many testing materials. Oppenheim illustrates a variety of techniques useful in measuring attitudes. The Center for Evaluation has sponsored a project known as MEANS. The project has, for example, compiled a listing of instructional objectives found in elementary schools and then appraised the tests available for measuring attainment of these objectives. More than one thousand tests or subtests have been looked at and evaluated for their validity, appropriateness for the child, usability, and technical excellence.

SAMPLING TO MAKE TEACHING
MORE EFFECTIVE

Traditionally teachers have given tests for two purposes: *grading*—giving grades to pupils as an indication to the pupil of how well he has performed on a task as compared to others—and *diagnosing*—determining the strengths and weaknesses of a learner in some instructional area, such as reading or mathematics. When one is testing in order to grade the pupil on the basis of his rank order with classmates, all take the same test, because it would not be fair to have pupils compete with each other if a test for one is easier than a test for another. The results of the diagnostic tests are supposed to suggest what should be taught if the learner is to progress. When testing for purpose of diagnoses, the test has to have enough different kinds of items to reveal the learner's particular deficiency—an achievement test suitable for grading is not usually sensitive enough, does not have discrete categories and enough items in each category to allow the teacher to know exactly where the learner is weak.

Recently a third purpose for testing has been getting attention: testing for the purpose of *assessing the effectiveness of instruction.* When doing this kind of testing, the teacher wants information as to whether or not a lesson, semester plan, or year's course of study has been successful. Unlike testing for purposes of grading and diagnosis, testing for feedback on teaching effectiveness does not require testing all pupils, and often the teacher will use the technique of sampling. For example, assume that a teacher has as his objective "given *ar* verbs in Spanish, the learner will be able to conjugate them in the present tense," and the teacher wants to know immediately after the lesson whether or not learners are able to conjugate as desired. However, to test all the pupils might take too much time, and to test the pupils on all *ar* verbs would be impossible. What should the teacher do? He should sample both pupils and items. If five pupils from a class of 30 are given a few *ar* verbs to conjugate and they do it correctly, the teacher can assume that the class has progressed. If none of the five can conjugate the *ar* verbs, he can be assured that his lesson was unsuccessful. Of course, the five pupils used as the sample should have been randomly drawn from the class as a whole (for example, calling on every sixth person as listed in the roll book, not just eager girls in the front row or five reluctant learners in the back row). Rather than giving the learners more than 4000 Spanish *ar* verbs to conjugate, the teacher randomly selects perhaps four or five. If the learners can perform correctly on these, the teacher infers that the objective (successful performance on the more than 4000 verbs) has been reached.

After every teaching lesson, evidence should be collected on whether or not pupils have acquired the competence specified in the objective. A sampling procedure will conserve testing time and preclude the arduous chore of correcting large numbers of papers. When evidence of attainment of the objectives requires observing learners engaging in a process or, for example, listening to the learner's oral production of speech, a sampling procedure is usually required. Seldom can a teacher monitor all learners closely enough in a single class period to check on the processes they are using. Nor can the teacher, at the end of a lesson, take the time to appraise the speech production (pronunciation of foreign words) of all pupils. By randomly selecting a few pupils and observing how they proceed when given a particular task or by asking three or four pupils to pronounce certain words, the teacher gets a good indication of whether or not his lesson was successful. Further, if a product such as a written composition or a paragraph is produced by pupils in the class, the teacher need not read all the papers to see if the products have the desired qualities. A sample of papers can suffice to indicate whether the teacher succeeded or failed. Similarly, it is wasteful of pupil time and expensive, too, for a school to administer achievement tests to all pupils when the purpose is to appraise teacher effectiveness. A sample of pupils can be drawn from a teacher's class, and their responses can indicate the progress of the class as a whole.

If one wants to know what the pupils in a class achieved as a result of instruction and the teacher has taught toward many objectives, a standardized achievement test will be an inadequate instrument, because the standardized test may not match the range of objectives taught. It would be better to have a pool of items—perhaps as many as 400 or more—which represent the objectives of the course. Any one pupil may be asked to respond to perhaps ten items at most (with items randomly assigned to pupils). The mean score at the beginning of the year—on the same randomly assigned items to the same pupils—compared with the mean score at the end of the instructional period will reveal whether or not there has been improvement in learner performance. This use of an item pool reduces testing time (it only takes a few minutes for pupils to respond to ten items), and the large pool allows more of the things taught in the classroom to be measured.

Sampling promises to make teaching more effective, because it can provide the teacher with frequent evidence that lessons are having the intended effect on pupil progress. The teacher need not wait until end-of-term examinations before knowing if his efforts are successful, and if there is immediate knowledge that the results are not satisfactory, the teacher is less likely to move on with his instructional sequences without first reteaching. Testing for purposes of diagnosis and grading does not provide the immediate and frequent feedback necessary for monitoring one's teaching performance.

DIFFERENTIATING INFERENCES FROM OBSERVATIONS

When engaging in inferential behavior, the student of teaching derives (from oral and visual observations) some idea that is not directly present in the observation itself. An inference is a logical derivation from what is seen and heard. In most cases, the one making an inference imagines himself in the position of the learner or the teacher observed and responds in accordance with the way he thinks the other thinks and feels. It is important that anyone looking at teaching recognize that there is a difference between observation and inference—that deriving the meaning in a teaching episode transcends the description of what is seen and heard. To make an inference one must be sensitive to subtle cues, ready to "put two and two together" in order to arrive at a new generalization. Inferences come when one draws on his own experiences in apprehending the deeper interpretations that lurk in the factual events recorded.

Test yourself on recognition of statements of observation and statements that are inferences by identifying the observations in the following:

> Teacher A has 18 boys to instruct in physical education. He wants the pupils to exhibit good sportsmanship. For 25 minutes he reads essays

written by sports idols, O. J. Simpson, Don Drysdale, and Mando Ramos. The boys are somewhat bored with the reading; they begin to talk during the reading. Next he has the class choose teams and lets them play for 30 minutes. Because the teams are not well balanced in ability, the games are not as challenging as they should be. Also, there are several instances of bad sportsmanship —one boy tells the umpire he made a mistake; another boy laughs when his peer awkwardly misses the ball.

The observations in the above paragraph include these facts:

1. There are 18 boys.
2. For 25 minutes the teacher reads essays written by three athletes.
3. The boys talk during the reading.
4. The class chooses teams and plays for 30 minutes.
5. One boy tells the umpire he has made a mistake; another laughs when his peer misses the ball.

Inferential statements such as "the boys are somewhat bored," "the teams are not balanced," "the games are not challenging," "there is bad sportsmanship" are interpretations. Interpretations are useful when accompanied by the observation which triggers their production, and a supervisor of instruction must learn to record the observations and then to make his inferences. Both should be shared with the teacher.

An outstanding examplar of a sensitive supervisor with highly penetrating and potentially useful inferences of teaching is found in the work of Goldhammer (1969). Unfortunately, we don't know how to develop in all students of teaching the capacity for gifted inferential judgments of teaching for which Goldhammer is noted.

RECOGNIZING THE PRINCIPLE
OF APPROPRIATE PRACTICE

One reason the principle of appropriate practice has gained recent popularity with instructional specialists is that it is a direct accompaniment to the trend toward more specific operational objectives. *Pupils must have opportunity to practice the kind of behavior implied by the instructional objective and to practice this behavior in the kind of situation specified in the instructional objective.* Without instructional objectives, there cannot be appropriate practice. Again, test yourself. See if you can select the paragraph(s) below which describe a teacher(s) using the principle of appropriate practice, assuming that each teacher has as his objective that the pupil will be able to identify propaganda techniques used in editorials in newspapers:

> *Teacher A.* He has the class spend at least one day per week discussing newspaper editorials he brings to class. These editorials often have propaganda material included. After the discussion each member of the class is given new editorials and asked to underline instances such as "card stacking," "bandwagon," and "appeal to fear."
>
> *Teacher B.* He has the class bring their own selection of editorials to the class each Thursday. Five students are chosen by the teacher to read their editorials aloud. After each reading the teacher as well as the class try to repudiate the point of view taken by the editorial writer, preferably by

nonpropaganda methods, although this is not required.

Teacher C. Teacher C reads extensive excerpts from propagandistic materials produced in Germany during World War II. He analyzes the material in such a way as to point out editorial techniques employed by the propagandist.

Only Teacher A is giving all students the opportunity to practice the behavior called for in the objective.

An excellent treatment of appropriate practice—which also distinguishes between equivalent practice (practice identical to the objective) and analogous practice (practice which demands the same covert or internal mental response as the objective but does not require the identical overt response)—is found in a programmed film strip available from VIMCET (1969). This instructional material also makes clear that a prerequisite task may contribute to attainment of an objective but that practice on a prerequisite task cannot substitute for appropriate practice calling for the behavior demanded by the objective itself.

chapter 6

APPLYING SUPERVISION
BY OBJECTIVES
IN STUDENT TEACHING

Individual teachers, elementary school principals, high school department chairmen, deans of instruction in junior colleges, supervisors of student teacher-interns and experienced teachers have been able to apply the behavioral model of supervision by objectives to their own needs in particular situations. The following describes uses of the model in student teaching.

SOLVING PROBLEMS IN STUDENT TEACHING

As reported in *Success in Teaching* (U.C.L.A. School of Education, 1968), there was a student teacher, Mr. J., of a beginning class in Spanish who was concerned that when given an opportunity to present a short, prepared recitation in front of the class, pupils were unwilling to do so. Mr. J. decided to work out a plan to change this recurring failure to participate, and his first statement shows this change as an instructional objective: "When giving an opportunity to recite in Spanish in front of the class, the learner will volunteer immediately." The teacher's own criterion was that at least three-fourths of the students would achieve this objective.

A pretest was unnecessary, because Mr. J. already had substantial information that his students were far from achieving the objective. Whenever he began recitation activities by asking for volunteers, the response was always negative. The problem was not merely that no pupil wanted to recite first—they didn't want to recite at all. Indeed, pupils had said they disliked this activity and participated only because they did not want their grades to be lowered.

Evidence that the objective had been reached would be when pupils raised their hands to volunteer to recite at the beginning of the recitation period and engaged in vehement overt behavior when volunteering (facial expressions and vocal efforts to attract the teacher's attention).

Observation and analysis by the supervising teacher revealed that Mr. J. rarely praised a pupil's recitation effort, but on the contrary usually made very deliberate corrections, perhaps to the point of causing embarrassment for some pupils in front of their peers.

Realizing that changes were necessary in his instruction, Mr. J. decided to find something he could praise in almost every recitation; yet he did not want to be so obvious that praise would seem insincere. Neither did he want to pass up the opportunity to criticize carefully with the hope that improvement would result. He decided to take notes on errors made during recitation and, afterwards, prepare written suggestions and distribute them to each student along with his grade on the recitation. The new procedure was announced to the class.

Within two weeks some improvement was noticed, but not as much as expected. Informal questioning of a group of his students gave an important clue: several of them said that they were not given sufficient time to prepare nor enough guidance from the teacher to avoid making errors. There was little opportunity for them to know in advance if what they prepared was correct.

Mr. J., therefore, devised a procedure whereby his pupils could be more successful in voicing correct Spanish. He made the recitation assignment one week ahead rather than a single day in advance, and he also planned two days of the week with no other home study assignments so that the time could be used by the pupils to perfect their recitations.

By the time of the third recitation period following Mr. J.'s new effort, he was gratified to see many pupils eager to recite. In fact, some pupils commented that they wished the recitations would hurry up and arrive. It was during the third recitation period that Mr. J. decided it was no longer of value to ask for volunteers, for almost the entire class was asking to go first.

In the above account there are instances representing essential aspects in the behavioral model for supervision: preassessment of learner performance, a specific instructional objective, data collection, a framework for analysis (praise, pacing, knowledge of results, error rate), and verification of the effects of teacher procedures by observing the consequences as shown in pupil performance. Whether or not Mr. J. was teaching to a valuable objective could be argued, but, the selection of an objective which calls for pupil cooperation and participation is at least common among teachers.

THE EFFECTS OF USING SUPERVISION BY OBJECTIVES

Forty-four student teachers in inner-city elementary schools were randomly assigned to "control" or "experimental" groups. Teachers in the control group were advised in writing that their grades in student teaching would be determined by their "professional characteristics and teaching methods." Factors to be considered were listed on an attached rating scale and included items such as appearance, maturity, classroom arrangement, and teaching procedures. Teachers in the experimental group were advised in writing that their grade in student teaching would be determined by their ability to select appropriate behavioral changes to be sought in learners and to effect those changes without undesirable by-products.

Pupils in the teachers' classes were pretested on skills of composition, and the results of this pretesting indicating the specific deficiencies found in each class were given all teachers. However, teachers in the experimental group were asked to stipulate prior to instruction what they would provide as evidence that they had helped pupils improve, while teachers in the control group were given instructions emphasizing the availability of authorized instructional materials which treated the development of the composition skills and were asked to submit copies of the lesson plans used in teaching these skills. In short, the control group focused on procedures and submitted written *plans*; the experimental group focused on results and submitted *criteria* for evaluating pupil change.

Post-testing of pupils revealed that pupils taught by teachers in the experimental group (emphasis upon results) achieved more than those taught by teachers in the control group (emphasis upon teaching procedures). Furthermore, the focusing of instruction upon overcoming a specific deficiency did not preclude pupils achieving desirable outcomes in other related areas.

A more complete account of the above experiment is available (McNeil, 1967), and indicates that the practice of supervision by objectives does not appear to produce undue pressure upon teachers. This is true at least under the conditions of this study, in which teachers determined objectives based on deficiencies of their own pupils and were not consciously competing with other teachers on a common test.

Many times in the past, merit ratings of teachers were based on the idea that two or more teachers would be compared by the relative gains of their pupils on a standardized test. This idea was resisted by teachers, because the pupils and teaching situations were not equivalent in the different classrooms and because the standardized test seldom reflected the actual teaching objectives of the teacher. In the experiment above, teachers in the experimental group stated their own objectives within the area of selected composition skills which they deemed appropriate for the pupils at hand. These teachers demonstrated their teaching power by advancing their pupils in the light of these objectives. The teacher was competing with himself by helping his own pupils regardless of other teachers and their work, and the consequence of the teacher's working for his own objectives was that pupils achieved more than they did when the teacher was instructed to follow specific procedures.

Replications of the experiment have been conducted with both student and experienced teachers. Some of these have been at the secondary school level (Moffett, 1966), and in foreign lands (Nwana, 1968; Smithman, 1970). In each case the results have been the same: pupils showed more gain when taught by teachers who established instructional goals and stipulated what would constitute evidence of pupil's attainment of these goals. There was also reliable evidence that teachers prefer to be evaluated on the basis of the progress evidenced by their pupils rather than by (1) ability to follow recommended procedures, (2) character—the extent to which one is a model for pupils, (3) ability to plan, or (4) ability to work well with the faculty.

STUDENT TEACHING NEW STYLE

Early in this book numerous weaknesses in programs of supervised student teaching were cited: supervising teachers do not have the technical specifications for participating in the improvement of instruction; student teachers are not evaluated fairly; there are no specific performance criteria for the student teacher, and instructional situations are not ordered so that the tasks of teaching can be more effectively mastered. These weaknesses can be overcome, and have been in some localities. The following is an outline of one way in which the correction can occur.

The supervising teacher (master teacher, cooperating teacher, intern advisor) must be given the chance to acquire the technical qualifications for participating in the improvement of instruction (see Chapter V for a description of these qualifications). The supervising teachers should be allowed to attend two or more formal inservice sessions treating the concepts and procedures necessary for technical competency and then practice using these techniques, conducting preobservational conferences, observations, analysis and strategy sessions, and postobservational conferences with their peers. This training should take place during the school day, and the practical problem of how to release teachers from their classes in order to participate in the training program can be met in various ways. One district engaged substitute teachers; another obtained special credentials for student teachers so they could "legally" remain with the class while the regular teacher participated in the training program. A third district developed its training program during a summer session when teams of teachers working with a common population of pupils were able to schedule periods freeing teams from responsibility for close supervision of pupils. The custodial assistance of volunteers (parents, resource persons), and the scheduling of special events (films, playground activities, and so on, which did not require the presence of one teacher with 30 pupils) have also been among the answers to the administrative problems of how to prepare the teachers without resorting to after-school, Saturdays or other penalizing procedures common to inservice education.

Central to the change in the supervisor's way of working with student teachers is recognition of the difference between the apprentice and the student of teaching. If there was little justification in days past for preparing teachers by having them imitate the methods of experienced teachers (apprenticeship), there is less merit in doing so at a time when the objectives of instruction are rapidly changing. An apprentice is handicapped, for he is wed to a particular method and does not have strategies for developing and verifying new methods to meet changing goals. The student of teaching, on the other hand, is prepared to define the results he seeks from pupils, to manipulate variables in order to maximize the attainment of these results, to see whether or not these results (and other by-products) occur, and to plan alternative approaches when particular procedures fail. Figure 4 is a characterization or report for prospective employers regarding a student teacher. The report presents the candidate as a student of teaching, not a dutiful apprentice. More attention is given to describing teaching competencies than personality independent of instructional effectiveness. The student teacher is rewarded for independence in getting results, deciding upon objectives, designing instruction, and monitoring his own performance.

A CONTRACTUAL SYSTEM FOR ASSESSING THE STUDENT TEACHER

Early in the student teaching assignment, student teacher and supervising teacher openly arrive at agreement on what constitutes evidence that the student teacher has or has not been successful. The student teacher has data indicating what pupils are now able to do with respect to the selected tasks and situations and has indicated how pupils will differ with respect to these tasks and situations in order to say that he has been successful. The student teacher is not required to write lesson plans or to follow prescribed procedures in reaching these objectives, but he is held accountable for the results which follow from his planning and the procedures he uses. Inasmuch as we want teachers who can get results and be students of teaching, the student teacher is expected to demonstrate mastery of certain "enabling objectives," such as ability to diagnose a learner's deficiencies in a content area and to make changes in his instructional sequences based upon results obtained from his work. If there are other criteria to be used in assessing the student teacher—criteria that are parochial in nature, for example, the personal "hangup" of a training teacher, such as a demand that the room be orderly before dismissal—these criteria, too, must be stipulated in advance of the teaching assignment. If the student teacher does not feel he should or can meet the private expectations of the supervising teacher, he should be given another assignment.

In the list below appear sample objectives for use with a team of student teachers.* Some of these objectives, such as 1, 2, 3, and 9, are "enabling objectives," necessary to fulfilling the role of a student of teaching. On the other hand, objective 17 emphasizes that the teacher must demonstrate that he can produce desirable results with pupils. Objectives 5, 6, 11, and 13 are representative of the kinds of peculiar demands made by individual schools and supervising teachers. Even though school and classroom policies and procedures often lack educational validation, adherence to them is a political necessity in most instances. For this reason the student teacher should at least know that these demands exist *before* starting to do student teaching. The student teacher and supervising teacher clarify this list of objectives before the assignment commences.

* Appreciation to Mr. Robert Otto and Dr. Leslie Shuck of the Newport-Mesa, Calif., Unified School system is gratefully acknowledged for their participation in the development of objectives for student teachers and for other suggestions in connection with teacher appraisal.

Figure 4 CHARACTERIZATION EMPHASIZING STUDENT TEACHER'S ABILITY TO GET RESULTS AND TO STUDY TEACHING

Miss Lamplighter

1. *Situation*

   A third grade class consisting of 35 Mexican-American boys and girls with an average IQ of 98, ranging from 64 to 112. In both reading and mathematics these children could work from first- to beginning third-grade level.

2. *Examples of Objectives Selected*

   a. Given printed words of one and two syllables which they have not seen before, children will be able to pronounce them. (75% of children will be expected to achieve this).

   b. Given most frequent phonograms in English (such as ing, ed), children will be able to pronounce them. (100% of children will be expected to achieve this).

   c. Given equations with single and two-digit numbers (such as $2 + \_\_ = 8$), children will be able to solve 8 out of 10 problems.

   d. Given multiplication problems, children will be able to demonstrate the use of repeated addition.

3. *Extent to Which Objectives Were Reached*

   Most changes sought, including those which demanded more than rote memory occurred without undesirable by-products (such as dislike of reading activity). Both bright and slow learners showed progress. Objectives in area of classroom participation (compliance with instructions) were not reliably reached. For instance, there were times when pupils did not follow directions and some children did not conduct themselves in accordance with classroom rules.

Figure 4 (continued)

4. *Evidence of Ability To Study Teaching*

There were many times when Miss Lamplighter incorrectly assumed that children had a background of experience necessary for successful participation, for example, children could not provide examples of terms used by the teacher in presenting the lesson. When pupils revealed the lack of the prerequisite, Miss Lamplighter usually (but not in all instances) designed a lesson to equip the learners (sometimes a single learner) with the prerequisite competency.

Evidence also was collected daily to indicate whether children had learned from the lessons. When lessons were not successful, Miss Lamplighter devised and carried out alternative plans using different materials and organization that (a) were thought to be more appealing to the pupils, (b) gave more examples, and (c) gave more opportunities for each child to practice the task.

At the beginning of the year most children had difficulty following directions. Hence Miss Lamplighter changed her manner of presentation to include fewer instructions at one time with provision for immediate overt response by pupils. Also she clarified her vocabulary by showing both verbal and visual examples. These changes in presentation resulted in about two-thirds of the class following directions reliably.

5. *Conclusion*

Miss Lamplighter has met the requirements of a beginning teacher. She has demonstrated ability to help most children achieve in reading and mathematics. She can analyze and revise her lessons on the basis of pupil response. She has not yet found how to enlist the cooperation of all pupils but is applying theories—manipulating instructional variables—that promise to be useful in dealing with particular pupils.

Grade   B+

**Objectives Held for Student Teachers
during Four Periods of Supervised Teaching:
Orientation, Assisting, Analyzing,
and Independent Teaching**

Objectives during Orientation

1. The student teacher will be able to state behavioral objectives which contain the following four characteristics:
   a. Identifies who is to exhibit behavior.
   b. Identifies behavior to be exhibited.
   c. Identifies the standard of performance (criteria).
   d. Identifies the given limitations and restrictions.
2. The student teacher will be able to formulate behavioral objectives in given curriculum areas for a class based upon preassessment data furnished by the master teacher. These objectives are terminal objectives to be met by the pupils during the time of the student teacher's training period. The supervising teacher must approve these objectives as a part of the total curriculum and be willing to teach to the same objectives during the assisting phase of the student teacher program.
3. The student teacher will provide the criterion measures (plan or instrument) for each behavioral objective stated in 2. The supervising teacher must agree that these criterion measures faithfully indicate attainment of the objective.
4. The student teacher must obtain an agreement from the supervising teacher and the other student teachers on his team upon the teacher criteria for each objective stated in 2.
5. The student teacher will be able to describe verbally, to the satisfaction of the supervising

teacher or principal, the policies and procedures of the school that have been identified as essential by the master teacher or principal at the beginning of the observation phase.

6. The student teacher will be able to describe verbally, to the satisfaction of the supervising teacher, the supervising teacher's classroom management policies and procedures that have been identified as essential by the master teacher at the beginning of the observation phase.

Objectives during Assisting Period

7. The student teacher will be able to diagnose an individual learner's deficiencies in a particular content area. The standard of performance in diagnosis demands that the student (a) prepare a task analysis of an instructional objective by which entry or prerequisite skills are identified; (b) select and develop measures for assessing the pupil's status with respect to these prerequisites; and (c) use these measures in assessing the pupil's status and from the data collected formulate objectives that promise to "close the gaps" identified.

8. The student teacher will be able to design an instructional sequence for the correction of a pupil's previously identified deficiency, a sequence at a specific objective. The student teacher should be able to provide a rationale acceptable to the supervising teacher for the sequence generated—for example, how it goes from simple to complex, how it gives appropriate practice in the objective itself, or how it takes into account the interests or values of the pupil at hand.

9. The student teacher will be able to make changes in his instructional sequence based upon results obtained from his work as tutor.

The student teacher will be able to state the basis for the change and why it is likely to improve results.

10. The student teacher will be able to operate in a classroom situation such equipment as an overhead projector, a tape recorder, a filmstrip and motion picture projector, or other audiovisual equipment used in the school.

11. The student teacher will be able to prepare transparencies and bulletin boards. The standards for work with these materials are to be determined by the supervising teacher.

12. Given the assignment to observe pupils during class sessions, the student teacher will be able to record verbal and nonverbal conduct of pupils and interaction patterns of pupils and teachers. He will be able to describe classroom situations and learners' responses to these situations, separating inferences from observations. Having made observations of pupils, individuals and groups, the student teacher will be able to formulate new instructional objectives based upon deficiencies inferred by data from the observations. These new instructional objectives must be acceptable to the master teacher and the other student teachers on his team.

13. Given pupils to direct, the student teacher will be able to maintain routine classroom procedures such as those of traffic, care of materials, and seating in the manner described and demonstrated by the master teacher.

Objectives during Appraisal Period

14. The student teacher will be able to perform all roles of appraisal team members—observer, analyst, strategist. Criteria for per-

formance include ability to make observations from lessons taught by peers, ability to analyze lessons using a number of instructional paradigms and principles, and ability to share observations with the teacher (student or master) who is observed, presenting negative inferences (properly labeled as inferences) for the teacher to consider.

15. The student teacher will be able to perform the role of teacher in a performance cycle (minilessons may be used as a context for demonstrating this competency). He will be able to collect preassessment data necessary for showing the appraisal team that objectives are warranted, to set teacher criteria for a given objective, to design and implement methods (means), and will be willing to test alternative teaching strategies and formulate new objectives from data and analysis presented by the appraisal team. The appraisal team is to be made up of the supervising teacher and the other student teachers.

Objectives during Independent Teaching Period

16. The student teacher will be able to design and execute lessons during a single day. The student teacher will be responsible for the total class for the day, although lessons may be differentiated for particular groups and individuals. These lessons should be conducted in accordance with the guidelines established, for example, pretest, strategy, setting of specific objectives, executing instructional strategy, and assessment of results.

17. The student teacher will be able to design and execute teaching plans extending over several days and in several content areas. Success of these plans and teaching effectiveness will be

indicated by post-test results on the last day of instruction given by the student teacher and by retention tests given by the master teacher.

The Student Teacher Demonstrates His Attainment of Objectives

As seen in the outline above there is a beginning period when the student teacher gets ready for teaching in a specific situation, a period when he acts as an assistant for the teacher, a period when he carries out the role of a student of teaching, and a period when he fulfills the essential teaching responsibilities of a credentialled teacher. Most student teachers can attain the above objectives if they are in the school throughout the day carrying no college or outside work for ten weeks. Each student teacher proceeds at his own rate. Usually the student teacher completes the first period in one or two days, the second period in one or two weeks, the third in three or four weeks, and the last period in from three to five weeks. At the elementary level, the student teacher generally works with a single class; in secondary school, the teacher works with perhaps five classes.

Both teaching and reflection upon teaching are necessary. The appraisal phase allows for analyses of teaching. By placing a team of three student teachers with the supervising teacher, one of the student teachers can accept responsibility for the class immediately after a lesson, thus freeing the teacher who has just taught for participation in a strategy session with the supervising teacher and a peer, who have participated in observing and analyzing the lesson. Unlike conventional student teaching, where student teacher and supervising teacher find it difficult to schedule a conference until the end of the day or before school the next day, the new plan (because of the team arrangement) allows for immediate help. The postobservational conferences are conducted in accordance with the procedures given on page 75.

There are special advantages to having members present through the day. When a team assignment is for only one or two hours in duration, there is less opportunity to perform a penetrating analysis and to cooperatively plan future lessons. Further, when opportunities to teach are limited, student teachers are less willing to forego teaching for analysis and planning. They do not want to perform the roles of observing and analyzing while a colleague has the coveted teaching role. On the other hand, when there is ample opportunity to teach, student teachers welcome opportunities to reflect.

chapter 7

APPLYING SUPERVISION
BY OBJECTIVES IN APPRAISAL
AND IMPROVEMENT
OF EMPLOYED TEACHERS

Do you recall some of the means for collecting evidence of "divergent" thinking, flexibility in problem solving and the like? There is, for instance, the practice of asking persons to list in a restricted period of time all the things one can do with a brick or to state various situations where a newpaper can be helpful. Some persons tend to respond in limited and conventional ways— "bricks are for building houses," "the newspaper for reading,"—others have more fertile imaginations. They can envision using a newspaper for polishing glasses, packaging fragile goods, and so on. Often those who score high on these "tests" are found among the economically poor who have had to adapt cheap and readily available materials in novel ways, using them as substitutes for more conventional but costly products designed for specific purposes. However, with training (usually in the form of practice and setting an expectation for novel responses), most persons can improve their performance by linking together solutions and problems which were not formerly associated. This chapter is written with a similar intention: the following cases are not only offered to be emulated but to stimulate the reader's own efforts at adapting the behavioral model for teacher assessment to his local problem.

A SCHOOL SYSTEM TRIES THE MODEL

A pilot study in Newport, California, sought to overcome the limitations of traditional assessment and improvement plans which focus upon the teacher—his personal characteristics, practices, and the like—without showing how these objects of concern make a difference to pupils—their achievements and predispositions (Newport-Mesa Unified School District, 1969). An underlying assumption was that no assessment and improvement program is complete unless it offers protection to pupils and evidences its power to increase the benefits of the educational program for pupils.

The Newport Study was an outgrowth from the work of a planning committee whose members had been appointed by the teachers' association and the school administration. This committee sought to evolve a plan for a unified approach to appraising teacher performance in the district. At the end of a year of study, the committee recommended trial implementation of an appraisal technique that would incorporate four major tasks:

1. Identifying current pupil status.
2. Setting goals and objectives for pupils.

3. Implementing means and materials to achieve goals.
4. Monitoring, analyzing, and evaluating the effectiveness of the means and materials.

The committee also proposed that staff in schools in the district volunteer for the trial. Approximately 100 teachers from five elementary schools and the faculty of the English and science departments of a high school participated in the study. These teachers represented a wide range of teaching experience, included first-year teachers and some with more than 27 years service.

Participants attended two 2½-hour sessions for the purpose of acquiring prerequisite tools, such as the ability to produce behavioral objectives. Then during the next two months the teachers formed teams and engaged in what were known as *performance cycles*. Three colleagues from a building, plus one person from outside the building constituted a team. Each member of the team had opportunities to play the roles of teacher, observer, analyst, and strategist. The cycles were typically carried out as follows:

1. The four team members met during a 30-minute session to conduct a preobservational conference where one of the members, who was to be the teacher in a forthcoming lesson, presented his objective to his team members. In addition, the teacher made clear what would constitute a satisfactory level of pupil performance and what percentage of pupils were expected to reach this level before the lesson would be considered successful.
2. During an observation phase, the team members collected data regarding the execution of the previously planned lesson.
3. Following the observation, the team of profes-

sional peers (without the presence of the teacher) compared the results of the lesson as shown by pupil achievement with what had been originally stipulated, reviewing the observation and analyzing the teaching performance. Although generalizations were drawn, no generalization was made without presenting the data which led to the inference. A strategy for conducting face to face sessions with the teacher was planned.

4. At a postobservation conference the teacher and his peers looked at results and derived alternative instructional procedures and objectives. Suggestions given the teacher came from interpretation of data, data which would have been difficult to acquire without the aid of trained observers.

When performance cycles were terminated, participants attended large group sessions where televised lessons and instructional problems were presented, affording opportunity for participants to demonstrate their ability to use the "tools" necessary for successful operation of the appraisal model. Opinions of the participants regarding the enterprise were anonymously expressed, and results showed that most teachers found the pilot study a worthwhile and stimulating experience. The teachers believed that their teaching had been strengthened and that consequently children learned more. They had increased their use of such practices as writing, objectives, pretesting, using knowledge of results, sampling, and giving pupils more appropriate practice and reinforcement. Participants began to focus on results rather than to prejudge methods, and they gave much more thought to what should be taught.

What conclusions were drawn from the project? It was demonstrated that the technique is effective, that supervision by objectives and the performance cycle reveal strengths and weaknesses in teacher behavior. For example, it was clear in several instances that colleagues were not selecting appropriate objectives for pupils. Some teachers displayed curricular weaknesses by teaching content which learners had already mastered. Other teachers showed instructional weaknesses such as trying to teach too much in a single lesson. (Children did not achieve until lessons were redesigned to teach to more sharply formed objectives.) The technique revealed those teachers who had no sense of direction—did not know what they were trying to accomplish. By contrast the procedures used permitted participants to identify those teachers who had formulated objectives of great importance both to the particular learner and to the society the school serves. Some of the objectives derived by the teachers treated the attainment of fundamental concepts in mathematics and reading; others emphasized the attainment of a process by which learners displayed that they were "learning how to learn." The latter included pupil question-asking behavior and positive predispositions toward situations calling for inquiry or problem solving. The supervisory techniques illuminated those teachers who had remarkable strengths in planning instructional strategies. There were teachers at both high school and elementary school levels who got intended results, often by taking a long-range goal and breaking it down (analyzing and sequencing the instructional task), identifying the prerequisites necessary for mastery of an objective.

ISSUES AND RECOMMENDATIONS

Several special issues and recommendations arose from the pilot study.

Validating Objectives

The technique worked better when teachers produced evidence in advance that their learners did not already have the competency called for in the objective. This practice, in addition to making the lesson a real test of the teacher's power to effect changes in learners, led to a better selection and more individualized selection of instructional goals.

Team Composition

Some participants expressed the opinion that unless a team has as one of its members someone from outside the building, there might be a tendency to become lax—to reveal only flattering descriptions of a teacher's act. Also, there was a belief that "inbreeding" might lead to an acceptance of low-level performance, that the use of technique might become a ritual. Indeed there was evidence among some teams that they were quite satisfied with the existing level of curriculum and instructional practice in the school.

The question of whether the principal should serve on the team—at least occasionally—was raised. Also, since team members differed in their competencies for discharging different roles, it was asked if all teachers should rotate in the roles of observer, analyst, and so on, or whether those with unusual talent for a role should perform that role consistently.

Honesty of Participants

Although the technique is designed to promote objectivity—for example the analyst must present data along with his inferences—it was apparent that some teams were more frank in supplying the teacher with the data and the resulting analysis. Some teachers were reluctant to share observations when they thought these observations and their implications would be painful to a colleague. There remained confusion in the minds of some about whether a team member should chiefly give encouragement and build the morale of the teacher or whether, in the interests of pupil welfare, he should be keenly analytical, "letting the chips fall where they may."

Assessment versus Instructional Improvement

There were teachers who wanted to emphasize instructional improvement and not use the information generated by the scheme as a basis for deciding whether the teacher should be retained. The idea of using a principle of complementarity in settling the argument was suggested. That is, there are times when the team centers upon helping a teacher improve his curricular and instructional effectiveness, and results in such a case need not be reported to the administration or personnel office. At other times the technique can be used to provide evidence that the teacher is or is not succeeding with pupils and that he is or is not doing something about his previously noted failures. Such information can be given to administrators in order to help them make a decision regarding the desirability of the teacher's remaining in the classroom.

It is important that all agree about whether the observation and recording of results is for the purpose of assessment or of improvement. Generally, assessment is best made by noting results obtained after a long period of instruction, but improvement can occur after lessons of 10 minutes or less have been analyzed. Frequent observations for the purpose of improvement should maximize the teacher's chances for getting desired results, and hence more favorable assessment.

THE PRINCIPAL AND HIS DUAL RESPONSIBILITY OF ASSESSMENT AND IMPROVEMENT

Role in Assessing

The principal has many alternatives in deciding how to discharge his dual responsibilities for assessment and improvement. The principal has the duty to recommend to the governing board that certain teachers should not be re-employed. As we have seen, principals rarely recommend dismissal, and when they do, it is usually on a basis other than pedagogical incompetence. Principals are fearful that their judgment regarding teaching effectiveness will not stand up in court should the teacher demand a legal hearing on the ground that dismissal should be "for cause only." Indeed, the principal often fears that he may be charged with *abuse of discretion*. Abuse of discretion is established if the principal's decision is not supported by substantial evidence. Prior chapters in this book have described a behavioral model for collecting substantial evidence regarding teaching effectiveness. It should be made clear, however, that the principal need not personally collect the evidence (although he may choose to do so). He can arrange for the supervision to be carried out by department chairmen or by teams of teachers. The findings of those employing the supervising model include data which when presented to the principal allow him to make decisions on teacher retention. When the behavioral model of supervision is used, the principal knows that there are facts available to support his decision should it be challenged.

A principal is remiss if he has not established and carried out a plan for monitoring the effectiveness of teachers as indicated by the quantity and quality of pupil progress. Just as he commonly relies upon secondary sources—complaints from parents, community members, and faculty gossipers—to influence his judgment of the teacher, so can he establish evaluative procedures to be sure that he is getting factual input about the teacher's ability to effect changes in learners, not mere subjective reports. A principal need not think that he has to observe the teacher personally in order to make a decision about the teaching strength and weakness of that teacher. In lieu of personal observation there are such alternatives as *delegation* and *product specification*.

Delegation is when others on the staff, because of technical qualifications (possession of subject-matter knowledge and skills of supervision), are asked to observe and analyze instruction. Staff members collect and present the data but let the principal make the decision regarding recommendation for retention of the teacher. The principal's decision can then take into account both facts about teaching effectiveness and the anecdotal (usually subjective) information regarding the teacher's conduct in areas other than instruction.

Product specification is necessary when a principal has a large number of teachers on his staff and when he himself is lacking in knowledge of the subject matter treated by the teacher. Years ago a principal could easily observe instruction of another, feeling quite competent to do so because he himself had taught in the same content field—a field then characterized more by stability than by the dynamism common to school subjects today. The principal thought he knew what procedures should be used in teaching something, and because of this his supervision practices were consistent with *activity specification*, not *product specification*. Activity specification is the practice of seeing whether a teacher is following a given procedure as directed; whereas product specification is specifying what the results (product) of instruction will be and then seeing what results occur. Under product specification one need not observe the process of instruction but can assess the outcome, noting whether it departs from the specifications agreed upon prior to instruction.

Product specification is agreed upon at a preinstructional conference between principal and teacher. Materials such as those issued by the U.C.L.A. Instructional Objective Exchange will greatly aid in selecting or formulating objectives to guide evaluation at the end of the year, the quarter, or whatever period of time the teacher has to demonstrate that he can teach, that he can make a difference in pupil behavior, or that his pupils can attain the instructional objectives.

Noninterventional measures, given before and after instruction, can indicate the changes produced by the teacher. For example, yearly comparisons can be made of the number and percentage of students who (1) continue with subsequent courses and achieve in the upper 25 percent of students in a subsequent course (2) attend classes daily, (3) promptly complete assignments, (4) start out and finish the course, (5) engage in extra activities stimulated by the class but which are not assigned and (6) care for and keep their class work and materials. Evidence of teacher effectiveness can be based upon observations of pupils' out-of-class behavior in given situations, for example, choices made in the cafeteria line before and after a course in nutrition. Projective devices yielding self-concept and morale scales which show the pupil's attitudes toward the class, the teacher, and the school are other examples of instruments available for observing the consequences of instruction.

A paradigm with criterion measures for evaluating instructional effectiveness has been prepared by Metfessel and Michael (1967). This paradigm lists indicators of status or change in cognitive and affective behaviors of students (1) on standardized measures and scales, (2) on informal teacher-made instruments, and (3) in noninterventional situations, such as frequency and type of disciplinary actions.

In addition to using techniques for determining whether or not a teacher has succeeded in achieving his instructional intents, evidence should be gathered to show that a teacher is or is not measuring up to the criteria associated with a student of teaching. The teacher should be observed as he participates in analysis and strategy sessions and as he formulates, tries out, and validates new objectives and instructional strategies.

Role in Improving Instruction

All principals believe they are improving instruction. Activities carried on under the rubric "improvement of instruction" are legion—everything from providing new materials and facilities to protecting the teacher from aggressive forces in the community comes under this umbrella. Not all principals, however, have accepted responsibility for (1) helping teachers make wise decisions about *what* to teach (curricular improvement) and (2) aiding teachers in their efforts to learn *how* to teach better (instructional improvement). The principal must either undertake these two tasks directly or arrange for others to do so.

An argument for the urgency of curricular and instructional improvement is found in a study by Bridges (1968), which revealed that elementary school principals, when considering a neophyte for a teaching position, give considerably greater weight to expressive characteristics than to instrumental characteristics of candidates. "Expressive characteristics" are those which deal with the kind of person the teacher is and his affect with pupils. "Instrumental" refers to the ability to perform the task of imparting subject matter and building the intellectual skills of pupils.

Principals are correct in giving first priority to selecting teachers who are high in the expressive dimension, because this kind of characteristic is not as amenable to change as behaviors in the instrumental dimension. A principal probably reasons that he can work with an expressive teacher and help him become better in instrumental acts, but that it is not so easy to help the instrumental teacher show more expressive behavior since such behavior arises from fundamental predispositions central to the individual's personality. Bridges' study takes on special import when it is recalled that, in a nationwide survey of elementary teachers conducted by the NEA, more than 50 percent of the teachers had only two observations during a nine-month term and fewer than half of the observations were followed by conferences. Limited supervision of the teaching act, when combined with emphasis on the expressive characteristics of teachers, provides little insurance against instrumental ineptitude in the classroom. "Under these conditions it is difficult to see how instrumental weaknesses get corrected and how teachers who lack instrumental qualities but possess strong expressive characteristics ever lose their right to teach."

Choices in Fulfilling Role in Curriculum Improvement
There is curricular improvement when teachers have

"better" instrumental intents—more appropriate objectives than before. Ways to recognize the relative goodness of objectives have been suggested on pages 89–93. The principal may use these procedures in helping the teachers either to formulate and to select new objectives or to justify the objectives now held. Many principals do not pretend to have the answer to the question, "To what end shall our instruction be directed?" They do not want to tell the teachers what the objectives shall be for particular learners or to play guessing games with the teacher, questioning until the teacher finally arrives at what the principal wanted from the beginning to be taught. Principals who are not certain in their knowledge of what to teach can still help the teacher to make better decisions about the objectives of instruction. How? One way is by looking at the teacher's presently held objectives and subjecting them to scrutiny, appraising them from a range of views—relevancy to pupils, utility in social situations, importance to a field, and others. Another way is to have the teacher give pupils preassessment measures revealing the learners' social behavior, subject-matter competency, and individual concerns. From these preassessment data teachers can then state where learners are and where learners should be, and the gap or deficiency between these two will suggest desired instructional objectives. Objectives arising from this process can in turn be subjected to review by principal and teacher.

Economical Use of Time   It is true that a principal can meet with a teacher during a preobservational conference prior to the teaching of a given lesson and help the teacher determine more valid instructional objectives, but with many teachers and many lessons there is not enough time for this. Therefore, instead of spending his time with the teacher on specific daily lessons, the principal might opt to help the teacher select valid instructional objectives for a longer period of time—several weeks, months, or a full year. He may believe that if objectives are valid for a school term, then there is a greater probability that the objectives for a day's lesson will also be more valid. The principal can also arrange for the teacher's colleagues to help with curricular improvement as they conduct the preobservational conferences necessary for observations of single lessons.

The principal uses his time more wisely if he discharges his curricular role at department or grade-level meetings (treating a single subject, such as primary reading). These meetings usually occur early in the term and take the form of individual teachers' presenting their preassessment data, the implications they have drawn from these data, and their tentative objectives, as well as ways in which they will collect evidence that objectives have been reached. The principal, along with other staff members, reviews the intents presented. A contract between principal and teacher is made when there is agreement that the objectives, the criterion measures, and teacher's expectations for individual progress are acceptable. The teacher and principal are then committed to the attainment of the objectives and to assessment of the teacher on the basis of whether or not these objectives are attained by the learners. Staff meetings for the purpose of helping teachers select objectives for the term are economical of time (the principal can help many teachers at the same time) and are often more effective with a given teacher because of group influence and support. Such a procedure allows a principal to know *what* his teachers are trying to accomplish as well as *why* they have chosen these objectives. Knowing and approving a teacher's objectives in advance of instruction provides the information necessary for a principal to discharge more effectively his other roles in support of the staff.

Choices in Fulfilling Role in Instructional Improvement
Suppose a teacher does not reach the end-of-term goals. Measures sometimes reveal performance judged as success in some areas and as failure in others, and these results suggest needed changes in teaching strategy. The principal may choose to help the teacher plan for the subsequent term by analyzing the results from the present, but a caution is in order: unless the measures used are comprehensive, there will not be enough information available to pinpoint where emphasis must be placed in the future. A standardized test seldom gives detailed enough information, and for this reason, some principals are now engaging in the practice of sampling larger numbers of items (problems, activities). For example, there may be as many as 400 items given at the end of a term, not merely the 40 or so that appear on a standardized test. Note, however, that no child is expected to complete the 400 items! Any one child might be given 10 of the 400 (learners do not take the same test when one is seeking to learn about performance on a wide range of situations).

Another example of an economical practice in testing for effectiveness of instruction, is when the principal randomly selects five or six pupils from a class, presents them with limited kinds of situations for which they are expected to be able to respond if instruction has been effective, and records the results. If the sample of pupils (all taking the same test) respond well or badly in some of these situations, then one can assume that the class as a whole would have performed similarly.

Help in instructional improvement should not await end-of-year analysis. The principal should establish opportunities for the teaching of minilessons using the four-phase supervisory model described in Chapter 4. The purpose of most of these lessons will be to reveal possible needs and ways for the teacher to improve (to suggest corrective actions). This purpose is in contrast to assessment of the teacher's power to effect change in learners where the emphasis is upon finding out whether the teacher did or did not get the desired results. Where the concern is improvement, teachers should be encouraged to attempt "high risk" objectives—those which they doubt their own capacity to effect. There should be no penalty for failure to get the results; rather, reward is given to the teacher's ability to recognize the failure, to analyze what was done, and to derive and test alternate strategies.

Although many principals will not be able to participate in all necessary preobservational conferences, observations, analysis and strategy sessions, and postobservational conferences, plans should be made for all teachers to participate in such activities for purposes of instructional improvement. Teams of teachers using the technical competencies defined in Chapter 5 can share the principal's responsibility for instructional improvement. The principal should, however, join these teams at least upon occasion. The following is an example of how a district might mandate an appraisal plan and how staff within schools might be expected to respond to the mandate.

District Memo to Schools

1.0 Mandate
That an appraisal plan (Model) for all District professional staff be implemented by (date).
2.0 Criteria for the Appraisal Plan to be developed by school.
    2.1 Allows for more persons than just the teacher to determine the quality of learning taking place.
    2.2 Makes it possible to eliminate a teacher when

it is shown that he cannot revise curricular objectives and instructional procedures when they are found wanting.

2.3 Makes it possible to eliminate a teacher if an agreed upon amount of stipulated learning of pupils repeatedly does not take place, and the teacher does not respond to improvement offered.

2.4 Does not provide an add-on cost once the plan is installed.

2.5 Provides data that will stand up in legal debates.

2.6 Provides a means of giving staff assistance to teachers where discrepancies have been identified.

Anticipated Response by School to District Mandate

School Appraisal Plan (Developmental Phase)

Purpose: Staff in the school will assess the teacher's ability to meet valid behavioral objectives and, at the same time, improve the quality of teaching.

Who Will Participate: All teachers on the staff of the school for the year are urged to participate in the Appraisal Plan. However, any teacher who prefers may request that he be evaluated by the traditional plan of the principal's classroom visitations. In the subsequent year, once a plan is tried and found to be acceptable, all teachers will be required to participate.

The Plan

1.0 Appraisal for teachers participating in the plan will consist of the following elements.

1.1 Teachers will work in teams of four, including the teacher to be appraised, and three fellow teachers assigned as follows:

1.1.1 First cycle—all appraisers same level (primary or upper) as teacher being appraised.

1.1.2 Second cycle—two appraisers same level as teacher being appraised, one appraiser from other level.

1.1.3 Third cycle—one appraiser same as teacher being appraised, two appraisers from other level.

1.1.4 At least one of the members doing the appraising should have technical competencies for participating in the improvement of instruction.

2.0 Operation of Appraisal Plan

2.1 District-supplied orientation will be provided for new teachers and returning teachers giving them training in technical competencies necessary for improvement of instruction.

2.2 Every school year each teacher in this plan will participate in two appraisal cycles of 2–8 weeks involving a different subject area. The first cycle is to be completed by Christmas and the second before Easter vacation. A third appraisal cycle will be held at the option of the teacher and/or appraisal team.

2.3 Steps to be completed in each appraisal cycle.

2.3.1 Each team will hold a preconference in order to assist the teacher in formulating and using the following elements: preassessment, precise objectives, validity of objectives, data to be collected, and analysis of lessons considering use of equivalent or analogous practice with activities related to the objective.

2.3.2 The teachers will collect the data that has been established in the preconference for personal feedback to see that the teacher being supervised is keeping on target and also for use in the post-conference, which is to be held with the members at the end of the time segment.

2.3.3 At the end of observation the team will hold a post-conference consisting of the following elements: reviewing and analyzing data collected by the teacher, trying to determine the "why" if objectives were not met, and forming new or revised objectives (see form that follows).

2.4 Any teacher having difficulty reaching his objective may feel free to call on the principal at any time for consultations, observations, or to participate in the preconference or postconference.

2.5 If the team feels a teacher needs more help in order to reach his objectives, they may also request the principal to participate in any or all parts of any appraisal cycle.

2.6 Each fall the teachers will select a person to get the Appraisal Plan started and monitor it throughout the year.

3.0 Recommendation to principal for re-employment of teacher on the basis of pedagogical effectiveness and ability to change teaching strategies when necessary.

3.1 The following form will be sent to the principal after completion of the second appraisal cycle:

Date_____

(Name of Teacher Being Appraised) has completed 2 cycles of the Appraisal Plan and (is) (is not) recommended for re-employment at this time in the School District.

Appraisal Team 1   Appraisal Team 2
1.   1.
2.   2.
3.   3.

(Signature of Teacher Being Appraised)

4.0   Report on observations.

Date _____

Teacher _____

Observers _____

4.1   Objectives — behavioral objectives selected jointly by teacher and observers.

4.2   Plan for measurement of attainment of objectives—agreement upon that which will constitute evidence that objectives have been reached, including statements of satisfactory level of performance for certain learners.

4.3   Data collected during observation.

4.4   Analysis of data—generalizations or comments with the data which led to the generalization.

4.5   Comparison of results obtained against the results expected.

4.6   New or revised objectives.

4.7   New instructional strategies to be tried and assessed.

chapter 8

EPILOGUE

Serious study of teacher accountability and of the behavioral model for supervision by objectives gives rise to several kinds of questions. Among them are questions about other supervisory practices and tools (What about self-analysis and videotaping?), adequacy of objectives and change produced (How much pupil progress is acceptable?), generalizability of change in teacher behavior (If a teacher improves in a given lesson, will all subsequent lessons be better?), and implementation (How does a plan for teacher accountability become a working reality?). To look at these questions and some answers should help clarify aspects of the particular supervisory model presented in this book and might trigger additional suggestions necessary for refining appraisal practices.

VIDEOTAPE IN THE SUPERVISION
OF TEACHERS

The technical development of the small portable videotape recorder has been used with a "minilesson" of four to eight minutes, taught to a "microclass" of five or six students, and with some scheme for analysis—usually that of interaction analysis. Sometimes the teacher focuses on trying some skill, such as a new questioning strategy or a particular pupil-teacher talk pattern. The lesson is taped, and the teacher analyzes his teaching by quantifying his behavior as recorded on the tape. The videotape is also used to show a teacher demonstrating some specific technique, such as how to use analogies and metaphors or illustrating "good use" of repetition in a lecture. Teachers viewing the model on the videotape hear prerecorded comments which call their attention to a specific aspect of teaching at the same time as the illustration occurs on the screen. The value of this directing or focusing comment, called a "contingent focus," has been shown by Young (1968). Once the specific teaching technique has been observed, teachers in training try to illustrate the technique themselves, and their subsequent trials are recorded and then reviewed by the participants.

Because of the many different ways in which videotaping is used in supervising instruction, one cannot say it is or is not generally helpful. A teach-review-reteach cycle usually brings favorable comment from participants. Teachers say they are helped in developing skills and that they find it interesting to see themselves and their pupils on tape. Much of the literature indicates that the videotape approach helps teachers see such things as personal mannerisms and appearance, the amount of talking they are doing, and their use (and misuse) of chalkboard and other materials. The greatest change in the teacher's procedures usually occurs between the first and second taping session, with very little change after that, and a teacher viewing his performance alone does not change as much as a teacher viewing his performance with a supervisor.

Because a videotape can be an excellent record—especially of nonverbal behavior—it has great potential. However, there is a "blind alley" to be avoided by those who would work with videotape and interaction analysis of instruction: the tendency for those viewing the tape and criticizing the lesson to assume that a given teaching style or procedure is "good" or "bad." The shared judgment of observers (valid or not) sometimes causes the teacher to maintain or to alter his procedures on the advice of others without validating this advice. I have tried to stress that a teacher or anyone else only *knows* if the procedure is good or bad by the consequences it produces with the learners at hand. When the videotaped record suggests procedures and teaching skills to be tried and checked out, it is serving a useful purpose, but when the record leads to teacher change without questioning the validity of the change, it is enslaving.

SELF-ASSESSMENT

We would like teachers to be students of teaching, assessing and revising their own teaching behavior. One theory holds that people want to evaluate to obtain an accurate picture of their own abilities (Festinger, 1954), many also desire to improve their teaching skills. An interesting aspect of the problem of motivation to improve is whether the teacher responds best to the feedback given by principal, colleagues, or pupils. Some teachers probably try to change in response to the expert assessment of authorities—words from the principal and statements from colleagues. Others are more self-directed in their learning, guiding their behavior on the basis of the consequences of their teaching as revealed by the actions of their pupils. Although supervision by objectives tends to strengthen the practice of a teacher who guides himself by task and results (progress of pupils) rather than responding solely to directions from the authority figures, the participation of such influential persons is not excluded. The principal, for instance, should participate actively in setting instructional goals with the teacher. Let's face it, most teachers require others "to keep them honest" and to provide help in solving their instructional problems. Without the opportunity for making collective judgment on instructional ends, some teachers would punish themselves (and their pupils) with unrealistic expectations. Because many instructional problems are highly complicated, they are better resolved when the intellectual resources of others are brought to bear, and it is also often more economical of time for teachers to work together on common instructional problems. This is true at least when the learning to follow from the experience is generalizable to the participants and to future instructional problems.

Teachers are most likely to change their classroom performance if they themselves see a discrepancy between what they want to achieve and what they are actually achieving. Supervision by objectives requires the teacher to confront himself *as a teacher*. Is he getting results or isn't he? Under this kind of supervision, the teacher cannot rest easy because he has presented lessons in what some believe to be an acceptable fashion but must verify his work against pupil growth. However, such verification does not preclude others' sharing experience with the teacher and providing him with the emotional support and anxiety (hopefully moderate) necessary for change.

No, it has not been shown that the teacher can best improve by viewing his own videotaped lessons in private, even if these lessons provide data of pupil performance and he is given guidelines for self-appraisal. The principal and staff can't take this easy way out but must establish a plan for more *public* assessment of the teacher's classroom technique to augment whatever *private* assessing the teacher is already doing.

To analyze one's own teaching and to work intensively on specific teaching strategies and content requires great commitment. Such commitment can be won by establishing and enforcing a school appraisal plan, which is especially necessary for those lacking in self-discipline. Review of the assessment and improvement plan and the way it is carried out should be made by representatives of the governing board, the administration, and the teacher organization. Unfortunately, in some schools there is tacit agreement between teachers and administrators that no one will "rock the boat." The faculty says their principal is fine, and he in turn praises the teachers. The staff really seems to believe they "have arrived" in their instructional expertise (are already good teachers), and all are very happy with their work, even to the detriment of the pupils. More encouragingly, there is evidence that the majority of teachers want supervision when clearly related to the progress and welfare of pupils.

TRIVIALITY OF OBJECTIVES

Assessment of a teacher in terms of results with pupils requires advance agreement by both teacher and supervisor on the appropriateness of the results sought. The setting of goals with a teacher is an instance of *contract decision*, a negotiated exchange between supervisor and teacher. The contract is renegotiable when the teacher has new evidence that an alternative objective is justified. The first time a staff tries contract decision, some teachers will state objectives that are not appropriate for various reasons, chiefly because learners have already attained them. One way to deal with this specific error is to ask the teacher to submit evidence that the learners cannot now perform as the objective requires, and before accepting a new objective, the supervisor may want to pretest and collect evidence showing how near pupils are to the objective.

Opposite to teachers with low expectations are those who set goals that would take years to gain, for example, a basic personality change. It is often fruitful in such a case to help the teacher make a task analysis—listing the prerequisite changes that would have to happen before the long-range objective could be reached. After the list is prepared, the teacher selects those changes which are both worthwhile and likely to be attained under the circumstances in which instruction will be offered. The teacher should be helped to identify the variables necessary for producing the changes desired and to compare them with the variables under his control—he must either gain access to the necessary conditions or give up the objectives.

Because instructional intents must be made operational, the supervisor and teacher can more readily identify and reject those which are indeed trivial. It is good to learn that important instructional intents in such highly aesthetic fields as painting and poetry can be made operational. Lindsay and Ambrose (1969), for instance, have prepared a number of behavioral objectives in poetry which they have derived from important generalizations in the field. The following are illustrative:

1. *Generalization:* Poems are not written primarily to communicate information. Predominantly their concern is with experience. A good poem conveys a fresh perception of life, gives the reader a heightened awareness and understanding of himself and his world.

    a. Given an unfamiliar poem containing a dramatic incident (Frost's "Out, Out—," for example) and a newspaper account that might have been written about the same incident, the student will write a paragraph contrasting the poet's way of looking at the event and the reporter's. A successful paragraph will develop adequately at least these points: differences in language, intent, and selection of detail.

    b. Presented with a literary selection, the student will point out orally examples (specific words, phrases, structural patterns) of the affective use of language.

2. *Generalization:* The basic part of the meaning of a word, its dictionary definition, is its denotation. The connotations of a word are what it suggests beyond its literal meaning—the feelings we attach to it because of our previous experiences with it. A good poet is sensitive to the feelings which surround words, to their connotations.

    a. Given a poem or a sample of "poetic" prose in which certain words or phrases conveying both literal and implied meanings have been underlined, the student will describe the connotations which each word or phrase evokes. He will support his answers by references to context.

    b. Given a line of poetry in which a word is substituted for the one the poet used, the student will be able to (1) explain how the substitution changes the meaning and (2) determine whether the alternative is better or worse than the original and why.

    c. The student will explain the connotations of specified words in an unfamiliar poem. He will describe the emotional response which the poet is trying to arouse by using the words.

3. *Generalization:* When a writer wishes to represent his experience to our imaginations, he uses sensuous language in preference to abstract or non-image bearing words. The poet conveys sense impressions by using not only visual images but images of sound, smell, taste, movement, internal sensations, and tactile experiences.

    a. Given an unfamiliar poem, the student will underline words which convey strong sense impressions. He will identify the image as visual, aural, tactile, and so on.

    b. The student will compose a paragraph describing an experience in which sound played a dominant part. A successful paragraph will contain words that strongly appeal to the sense of hearing and will include details that are sharp, vivid, and concrete.

    c. Given an unfamiliar poem, the student will (1) explain the concrete images (What do you see as you read?), (2) state the abstract idea which each image expresses, and (3) describe the feeling attached to the image.

4. *Generalization:* When we speak or write, we make two kinds of statements, literal and figurative. A poet uses a figure of speech—meta-

phor, simile, personification, for example—when he wants to say one thing and mean another.

   a. Given an incomplete simile and several alternative completions, the student will choose the ending which most nearly meets the criteria of suitability and freshness or surprise.

   b. The student will point out orally words or phrases in a literary work that ascribe human or animal traits to inanimate objects. He will describe the effect of the personification.

   c. Given metaphors or similes in context, the the student will be able to state orally or in writing (1) what things are being compared, (2) how they are alike, (3) the literal meaning of the metaphor or simile, and (4) its abstract or symbolic meaning.

5. *Generalization:* In poetry, as in music, sound and rhythm help create the total meaning, the effect the poet wishes to have upon the reader's imagination.

   a. Given two poems in which patterns of sound and rhythm contrast sharply ("Velvet Shoes" and "The Highwayman," for example), the student will cite specific reasons for the different effects (for example, long or short vowel sounds, liquid or harsh sounds, predominance of monosyllabic or multisyllabic words). He will further explain how the sounds and the rhythmic patterns which each poet has selected contribute to the total effect.

   b. In specified lines of a given poem, the student will describe the relationship between the sounds of the words and their meaning. He will validate his statements by refer-

> ence to the situation in the poem, its tone, or its total meaning.
>
> c. Given an unfamiliar poem the student will (1) describe in writing the kinds of rhyme the poet uses and (2) explain what effect he is trying to achieve by this kind of rhyme. He will support his interpretation by evidence from the poem.

Supervision by objectives permits one to look at both predicted and unforeseen consequences, because having an initial list of objectives often directs attention to a more comprehensive set of consequences than would otherwise be noticed. In some schools each teacher will select objectives that include behavior in different categories—cognitive, affective, and motor—and demand several levels of learner responses—for example, recalling, applying, synthesizing. Reward for attempting the difficult can also be given, if the plan for assessment provides a "bonus" for the teacher who reaches a "high risk" objective and if the teacher is told that he will not be punished if he fails to reach the difficult objective.

Once more the reader is reminded that when assessing a teacher's instructional power, he should give first priority to getting the results desired. On the other hand, when instructional improvement is the focus, getting results is not as important as deriving new strategies in the face of disappointing results. The teacher and supervisor must be clear about when they are putting results uppermost (assessing power in teaching) and when they are giving teacher problem-solving behavior primary attention (improving one's instruction). Both are necessary, but they require different procedures. When assessing a teacher's power in teaching, we tend to reward him for getting results, when improving instruction, we reinforce the teacher's efforts at analyzing and redesigning lessons.

AMOUNT OF PUPIL PROGRESS NECESSARY

How much progress must a class show before the teacher can be declared successful? The answer to this question leads to the conclusion that evaluation of instruction is essentially a subjective decision. We can measure the fact that change in learner behavior has occurred from teaching, but deciding how much change should be expected is a judgment to be made by teacher and supervisor. In some instances, it may be sufficient to show that there is a statistical difference in pre- and posttest scores, or it may be enough to prove that there has been *no loss* of pupil interest in the subject between September and June (morale scores generally decline during a year). There are expectancy tables for learners with given characteristics (e.g., IQ, age, socioeconomic level), indicating normative achievement on selected tasks. Adjustment of levels of expectation might follow the recognition of circumstances present in the classroom, such as unusual group dynamics and a skewed population of learners. However, I would like to think that we are moving away from the practice of comparing achievement levels in one class with achievement levels in other classes, because this practice with its frequent use of standardized tests and normative data has many weaknesses. Two more fruitful approaches are:

1. Use criterion-referenced measures (Glaser, 1963). Observe how learners are able to perform the specific tasks implied by the objec-

tives. Such measures indicate the content of the learner's behavioral repertory and the correspondence between what he can do at the beginning and end of instruction, independent of reference to the performance of others. This is in contrast to norm-referenced measures, which are designed to tell that one student is more or less proficient than another (relatively) but do not give much information about the absolute degree of proficiency exhibited. The latter might be all right if one is more interested in grading the student than knowing whether or not objectives are reached.

2. Assume that a large percentage of pupils in a given class can reach mastery of the objectives and reward the teacher as he increases the percentage of pupils reaching mastery (increase in percentage to be indicated by comparison with numbers of pupils achieving mastery in former classes of the teacher with those in the present class).

Benjamin Bloom's "Learning for Mastery" (1968), illustrates what is meant by the above admonition. Unlike many teachers, who expect about a third of their students to adequately learn what is taught, Bloom has aspired to have most (90 percent) master the subject under consideration, and he sees his job as that of finding the means that will enable the largest proportion of pupils to attain mastery. In one course Bloom used parallel achievement tests in 1965, 1966, and 1967. In 1965, before adopting a particular teaching strategy, "Learning for Mastery," approximately 20 percent of the students received a grade of "A" on the final examination. In 1966, after the new teaching strategy was employed, 80 percent of the students reached the same level on a parallel examination and were given the grade of "A." Results in

1967 showed that over 90 percent of the students achieved mastery and were given grades of "A."

Bloom's approach is to supplement regular group instruction with diagnostic procedures and alternative methods and materials in such a way as to bring more pupils success. He attempts to spell out some of the preconditions necessary for specifying the objectives of instruction and selecting evaluation instruments. Both teacher and learner have an understanding of what the achievement criteria are, and both collect evidence of progress toward these criteria. Students do not compete with each other for grades; they receive grades on the basis of individual level of performance, not by rank order in the group—hence students work cooperatively with each other without being concerned about giving special advantage to peers. Bloom's course is divided into small units of learning, each composing a week or two of learning activity, and these units are sequenced into a hierarchy of learning tasks. Brief diagnostic progress tests are used to determine whether or not the student has mastered the unit and what, if anything, the student must still do to master it. Frequent tests pace the learning of students and help motivate them. The use of tests also helps insure that each set of learning tasks is thoroughly mastered before subsequent learning tasks are started. The work from students who lack mastery of a particular unit is analyzed, revealing the specific questions answered incorrectly and the skills and processes the students need to work on. Students are then referred to particular instructional materials intended to help them correct their difficulties—diagnosis is accompanied by specific prescription. Students are not given letter grades on these short checkup tests, since the purpose of these tests is to guide improvement and to give the teacher feedback regarding the success of his teaching. As a technique for correcting a deficiency, Bloom has found it beneficial for small groups of students (two or three) to meet regularly for an hour a week to view the results of their checkup tests and to help each other overcome the difficulties identified on these tests.

By my standards, Bloom can be identified as an outstanding teacher both in terms of power to effect change and willingness to study his teaching. His results are impressive—yearly improvement as shown by percentages of pupils achieving mastery (20 percent to 80 percent to 90 percent). Furthermore, he meets the specifications of a student of teaching. He tries new strategies (such as use of tutors, use of programmed texts, use of selected audiovisual materials, use of checkup tests), and he validates these new departures. He does not assume that there is a single strategy for mastery. He has many lessons that are failures; however, he *knows* when these failures occur and does something about them. He has evidence, for instance, for which student a teaching procedure has not proven effective and in the light of this takes it upon himself to provide an alternative procedure to the learner.

VALUE IN ANALYZING A SINGLE LESSON

The spontaneous act of live classroom teaching differs from a preplanned teaching instrument, such as a textbook, programmed lesson, or film. A teaching instrument is reproducible in two senses: (1) the instrument itself can be copied (reproduced) in numbers, and (2) the results obtained from the use of the instructional material can be quite consistent when the material is used with a common population of learners under similar conditions (reproducibility of effect). It is, therefore, economically beneficial to work at improving teaching instruments, by trying them out and revising them in the light of the findings so that the instructional "package" gets better results in less time. Unlike a programmed lesson which will be used many times in thousands of situations, the teacher usually presents a lesson once to a single class or to four or five classes. Teachers might wonder then if it is worth the time to rehash that lesson which won't be taught again until next year, if at all. One misses the point, however, if he thinks that analysis sessions and postconferences are for the single purpose of improving a teacher's given lesson. The purposes for analyzing a teacher's lesson are different than the purposes served by analytical and empirical studies of reproducible programs. For one thing, the teacher is not so concerned with bettering a particular lesson which has just been taught but is more interested in designing a new lesson—a subsequent lesson with its own objectives and procedures. As stated previously, the teacher should try to leave a post-observational conference with new objectives and new teaching strategies to be tried in forthcoming lessons. In addition, there may have been some teaching practices revealed in the particular lesson observed that are generalizable to many future lessons, such as increased use of praise or modified question-asking behavior, etc. If it is believed that one of these practices made a difference in the learning of pupils upon one occasion, the teacher should consciously manipulate and test this practice in other lessons and with other pupils.

INTRODUCING A PLAN FOR ASSESSMENT AND IMPROVEMENT OF TEACHERS

There is considerable literature regarding ways to effect changes in schooling (Miles, 1964) and (Carlson, 1965). The introduction of a plan for assessment and improvement into an eduational organization can occur in a variety of ways. It can originate with the administration, and the superintendent and principal are key figures in the innovative process at the local level. However, because the classroom teacher will play an important role in getting the plan to work, it seems logical to equip teachers with the qualifications necessary for participating in assessment and improvement before asking them to fulfill their new roles as assessors and analyzers. Both beginning and experienced teachers can participate effectively in making the plan a success (Bridges and Reynolds, 1968). Support and leadership from teachers' organizations might also be important in launching the plan and in monitoring its enactment, and some school systems will find the participation of parents and other consumers of the educational product not only helpful but necessary.

Development of an appraisal and improvement plan is a worthwhile educational activity because such a plan is fundamental to the future of the school, not an appendage. Throughout the land the climate for introducing appraisal plans is right. National interest in improving education has generated a host of related projects under such rubrics as "performance criteria," "programmed budgeting," "quality control," and "national assessment." Those responsible for teacher preparation have begun to recognize the inadequacies of present procedures in evaluating student teachers. As reported in Chapter 1, there is general dissatisfaction on the part of school administrators, leaders of teachers' organizations, and teachers themselves with how teachers are judged and helped.

The public would welcome a plan that leads to both more warranted instructional outcomes and higher achievement among larger numbers of students. To this end, citizens are not antagonistic to provisions for making teachers more responsible for the quality of learning of pupils. There are teachers, however, who will resist the introduction of procedures by which they are held accountable for results. A survey by the National Education Association showed that most teachers think they should be evaluated although they differ in their views as to the purpose of the evaluation. According to those conducting the survey nearly 93 percent of responses from the population of teachers in the survey favored undertaking evaluation to assist in improving teaching competency while 54 percent of the responses were favorable to using evaluation for the purpose of making it possible to dismiss poor teachers (NEA 1969).

One way to lessen teacher opposition is to have a plan which not only features pupil growth as the ultimate criterion for judging teacher competence, but includes improvement procedures which promise to help the teacher find success in getting the desired results. Many so-called instructional improvement activities and changed working conditions for teachers have not been introduced by first specifying how these innovations will enhance the achievement of pupils. By designing and using procedures for teacher improvement in accordance with the guidelines given in the present text, the teacher receives the kind of help that maximizes attainment of contracted responsibility.

Teacher acceptance of an accountability plan requires assurance that parallel to holding the teacher responsible for results there be provisions that promise the teacher a good chance to attain desired results. Information showing that the teacher has failed to produce specified change in pupils during improvement sessions should be used for deciding how to help the teacher, not for deciding whether or not to fire. On the other hand, the teacher must understand that an accountability plan is not solely for the purpose of improving teacher behavior. The teacher must accept the fact that there will be occasions when information regarding the teacher's impact upon the student will be collected primarily to serve as a basis for deciding upon the teacher's promotion and retention.

References

Allen, Dwight, and Kevin Ryan. *Microteaching*. Reading, Mass.: Addison-Wesley Publishing Company, Inc., 1969.

Amidon, Edmund, and Neal Flanders. *The Role of the Teacher in the Classroom*. Minneapolis: Paul S. Amidon and Associates, Inc., 1963.

Anthony, Bobbie M. A New Approach to Merit Rating of Teachers. *Administrator's Notebook*, XVII, 1; September 1968.

Association for Supervision and Curriculum Development. *Better than Rating*. Washington, D.C.: the Association, a department of the National Educational Association, 1950.

Ayers, Leonard P. Measuring Educational Proccesses through Educational Results. *School Review*, XX:300–319; 1912.

Bain, Helen. Self-Governance Must Come First, Then Accountability. *Phi Delta Kappan*, LI, 8; April 1970.

Bellack, Arno A. The Language of the Classroom: Meanings Communicated in High School Teaching. In *The Nature of Teaching*, ed. by Lois N. Nelson. Waltham, Mass.: Blaisdell Publishing Company, 1969.

Bixler, Ray H. Ostracize Them. *Saturday Review* 47–48; July 2, 1966.

Bloom, Benjamin S. (ed.). *Taxonomy of Educational Objectives, Handbook I, Cognitive Domain.* New York: David McKay Co., Inc., 1956.

Bloom, Benjamin S. Learning for Mastery. *UCLA–CSEIP Evaluation Comment*, 1, 2; May 1968.

Boyce, Arthur Clifton. Methods for Measuring Teachers' Efficiency. *The Fourteenth Yearbook of the National Society for the Study of Education.* Chicago: University of Chicago Press, 1915.

Bridges, Edwin M. *Preferences of Principals for Instrumental and Expressive Characteristics of Teachers Related to System Type.* Paper presented before the American Educational Research Association, Chicago, Ill., 1968.

Bridges, Edwin M., and Larry B. Reynolds. Teacher Receptivity to Change. *Administrator's Notebook*, XVI, 6: 1–4; February 1968.

Brown, Bob Burton, and William Nicholas Stoffel. *Some Effects of Observers' Beliefs on Classroom Observations of Teachers' Behavior.* Paper presented before the American Educational Research Association, Chicago, Ill., 1968.

Buros, Oscar Krisen (ed.). *The Sixth Mental Measurements Yearbook.* Highland Park, N.J.: The Gryphon Press, 1965.

Carlson, Richard O. *Adoption of Educational Innovation.*

Eugene, Ore.: Center for the Advanced Study of Educational Administration, 1965.

Cohen, Arthur M., and Florence B. Brawer. *Measuring Faculty Performance.* Washington, D.C.: American Association of Junior Colleges, 1969.

Dalis, Gus T. *The Effect of Precise Objectives upon Student Achievement in Health Education.* Doctoral thesis. Los Angeles: University of California, 1968.

Dewey, John. *The Sources of a Science of Education.* New York: Horace Liveright, 1929.

Festinger, L. A. A Theory of Social Comparison Process. *Human Relations,* 8:117–140; 1954.

Gage, N. L. An Analytical Approach to Research on Instructional Methods. *Phi Delta Kappan,* XLIX, 10:601–606; June 1968.

Gagné, Robert M. *The Conditions of Learning.* New York: Holt, Rinehart and Winston, Inc., 1970.

Glaser, Robert. Instructional Technology and the Measurement of Learning Outcomes: Some Questions. *American Psychologist,* 18, 7:519–521; 1963.

Goldhammer, Robert. *Clinical Supervision: Special Methods for the Supervision of Teachers.* New York: Holt, Rinehart and Winston, Inc., 1969.

Hilgard, Ernest R. *A Basic Reference Shelf on Learning Theory.* Palo Alto, Calif.: Stanford University, ERIC Clearinghouse on Educational Media and Technology, 1967.

Hughes, Marie M. *A Research Report—Assessment of the Quality of Teaching in Elementary Schools.* Salt Lake City: University of Utah, 1959.

Krathwohl, David R., Benjamin S. Bloom, and Bertram B. Masia. *Taxonomy of Educational Objectives, Handbook II, Affective Domain.* New York: David McKay Company, Inc., 1964.

Lindsay, Marilyn, and Freeman Ambrose. *Objectives for What Poetry Means.* Los Angeles: Office of Supervised Teaching, UCLA, 1969.

Mager, Robert F. *Preparing Instructional Objectives.* Palo Alto, Calif.: Fearon Publishers, 1962.

McNeil, John D. Concomitants of Using Behavioral Objectives in the Assessment of Teacher Effectiveness. *The Journal of Experimental Education,* 36:69–74; 1967.

Medley, Donald M. Experiences with the OSCAR Technique. *The Journal of Teacher Education,* XIV:267–273; September 1963.

Metfessel, N. S., and William B. Michael. *A Paradigm Involving Multiple Criterion Measures for the Evaluation of the Effectiveness of School Programs.* Paper presented before the American Educational Research Association, New York, 1967.

Miles, Mathew, B. (ed.). *Innovation in Education.* New York: Teachers College Press, 1964.

Moffett, George McHatton. *Use of Instructional Objectives in the Supervision of Student Teachers.* Doctoral thesis. Los Angeles: University of California, 1966.

Morsh, Joseph E., and Eleanor W. Wilder. *Identifying the Effective Instructor: A Review of the Quantitative Studies 1900–1952.* Chanute Air Force Base, Ill.: Air Force Personnel and Training Research Center, Project 7714, 1953.

National Education Association, Research Division. *Evaluation of Classroom Teachers.* Research Report 1964–R14. Washington, D.C.: The Association, October 1964.

National Education Association, Research Division and the American Association of School Administrators. *Evaluating Teaching Performance.* Educational Research Service Circular 3, 1969. Washington, D.C.: The Service, May 1969.

Newport-Mesa Unified School District. *Staff Performance Appraisal Plan Pilot Study 1968–69.* Newport Beach, Calif.: The Development Lab., 1969.

Nwana, Elias Muthias. *An Investigation into an Objective Way of Examining Student Teachers in Practical*

Teaching in West Cameroon Teacher Training Institutions. Doctoral thesis. Los Angeles: University of California, 1968.

Oppenheim, A. N. *Questionnaire Design and Attitude Measurement.* New York: Basic Books, Inc., 1966.

Popham, W. James. Probing the Validity of Arguments against Behavioral Goals. In *Current Research on Instruction,* ed. by Richard C. Anderson and others. Englewood Cliffs, N.J.: Prentice-Hall, Inc., 1969.

Rosenshine, Barak. *Objectively Measured Behavioral Predictors of Effectiveness in Explaining.* Paper presented before the American Educational Research Association, Chicago, Ill., 1968.

Segure, Rolfe. Union Offers New Rating Plan. *Los Angeles Times,* Part II: 8; Sept. 23, 1966.

Silberman, H. F. *Experimental Analysis of a Beginning Reading Skill.* Santa Monica, Calif.: Systems Development Corporation, 1964.

Smith, B. O., and others. *Teachers for the Real World.* Washington, D.C.: American Association of Colleges for Teacher Education, 1969

Smithman, Harold H. *Student Achievement as a Measure of Teacher Performance.* Doctoral thesis. Los Angeles: University of California, 1970.

Sorenson, Garth. What Is Learned in Practice Teaching? *The Journal of Teacher Education,* XVIII, 2:173–178; Summer 1967.

Tyler, Ralph W. *Basic Principles of Curriculum and Instruction.* Chicago: University of Chicago Press, 1965.

U.C.L.A. School of Education. *Success in Teaching.* Los Angeles: University of California, Los Angeles, 1968.

Vimcet Associates. *Appropriate Practice.* Los Angeles: Vimcet Associates, P.O. Box 24714, 1969.

Wickman, E. K. *Children's Behavior and Teachers' Attitudes.* New York: The Commonwealth Fund, Division of Publication, 1928.

Wittrock, M. C. Set Applied to Student Teaching. *Journal*

of *Educational Psychology,* LIII, 4:175–180; August 1962.

Young, David B. *The Effectiveness of Self Instruction in Teacher Education Using Modelling and Video Tape Feedback.* Paper presented before the American Educational Research Association, Chicago, Ill., 1968.

Index

A

Abuse of discretion, 132
Activity specification, 134
Ambrose, Freeman, 153
Anderson, Robert H., 51
Assessment of teacher competency
  based on ability versus other factors, 28
  as evidence for dismissal, 131, 156, 163
  versus instructional improvement, 52, 131, 156, 163
  nonintrusive measures of, 134
  prizing versus appraising in, 13
Ayres, Leonard P., 16

B

Bain, Helen, 24
Behavioral correlates of teaching effectiveness, 68
Bloom, Benjamin, 159
Boyce, Arthur, 17